The Retail Leader

"It's Not About You!"

The Retail Leader

"It's Not About You!"

Jeffrey Hester

The Retail Leader

Copyright © 2019 by **Jeffrey Hester**

Printed in the United States of America

First Printing, 2019

ISBN: 978-107917686-5

Whiptail Publishing

The Retail Book 16996 w Hammond st. Goodyear, AZ 85338

www.TheRetailBook.com

Dedication

This book is dedicated to the thousands of associates I have worked with as a peer, as a supervisor, as a manager, as a teacher, as a coach, and as a leader in my retail career up to this point and in the future as well. I would not be where I am or have the experiences to share would it not have been for the great people that I have had the opportunity to work with and the horrible people whom I have had the displeasure of working with, as well, who have all made me a better leader. Because of them, I am better able to adapt and can overcome any situation thrown my way. I truly believe it is my role to pay back all the great things I have in life and in my career, and this is the best way to do so on a wide scale.

I also want to dedicate this book to my wonderful wife and daughter who have put up with crazy schedules at work during the past 17 years, the 6- or 7-day work weeks it takes at times, the stress and venting I bring home when I face a tough problem at work, and ultimately supporting me every step of the way-- regardless of all that--so that I could pursue my retail leadership career. I love you more than anything, and I thank you for the support you have always shown to me!

I do what I do for my associates to help them build better lives for themselves and now, writing this book, I did that for you the reader as well, so you can build a better life for yourself! Thank you for buying this book and taking the first investment in your future. I wrote this book with you in mind. The chapters are easy to read quickly so you can come back to them repeatedly, as needed, and not have to re-read from start to finish. I hope this book will allow you to take everything you know--or think you know--and add value by helping you build an arsenal of tools in your leadership toolbox.

Contents

Introduction

I wrote this book after almost two decades of hands-on, real-life experience in a retail leadership role. I started at the bottom of the totem pole, so to speak, pushing shopping carts and loading customer's vehicles part time. As of this writing, I oversee an entire district worth of team and have more than $750 million in retail sales under my leadership.

When I first started out I was pushed into a leadership role by management at that time, and with no training to hit the ground running. As a result, I had wins and losses and struggled more than I would have liked, even though as a whole I was delivering on results and expectations put in front of me. Had I been able to give myself a head start by reading up on a few topics I wasn't yet comfortable with to obtain a higher level understanding of things that I would come across in my career, I absolutely would have taken advantage. Unfortunately, I couldn't find anything that wasn't purely motivational mindset junk, or something written to coach you on being a CEO or leader at only the top level. I knew there was a need for something that could help people either new in position or seeking a promotion into that first leadership role. I hadn't given it a thought again until recently when I decided to start writing a training manual of sorts for my team of leaders who always had the same questions and the same problems with their new leadership roles.

I coach and train new retail leaders every day in my current role and have used every tip and trick in this book to help set up my mentees for success, so they have a better chance at success than 99% of those who go into a new leadership role with no mentorship, coaching or training. I have been fortunate enough during my career to have been talented in my role as a leader in certain areas and have been able to grow my skill sets in areas in which I wasn't the strongest. With this book, you will be able to expand your own talents and grow additional skills that you may not have ever even considered. The tips and tricks in this book can be used by those seeking a leadership career, by brand-new leaders, and even by leaders who have been in their position for years. I think all leaders should constantly look to improve their leadership skills, regardless of how good they think they are, and I assure you that you will be happy with the result when you start to put this knowledge to work.

I applaud you for looking to develop yourself and your future career and hope you find many things in this book that will help you prepare for your first position, to grow in your current role, and to continually develop your leadership skills and abilities over the course of your career. I wrote this book for people like you, and I hope that you find it as valuable as the leaders whom I have developed in the past. Please share what you learn with others and make yourself a true retail leader.

Chapter One
Why Me, Why Now?

Whenever I sit down with a new prospect for one of my leadership positions in my store I always ask them a simple question. Why you, why now? This may seem like a silly question to many, and the answer is easy: "I want more money, I want more power, I want to prove myself," right? Wrong! I am looking for honest answers which show they are looking for more than just money and a title. I am looking for them to tell me about what they plan to do with the position, what they've done up to this point to train themselves and learn as much as possible, so they will come into the position running instead of crawling and struggling to learn what it takes to truly be a leader and not just a figurehead manager. This book will help you to answer this question not just for an interview, but for yourself, so you can truly determine if being a manager or leader is truly the best position for you. It will help you assess your comfort levels with authority, autonomy, decision making, accountability, motivation, game planning, recognition, rewards, retention, hiring, terminations, promotions, development, and the list goes on and on.

I can tell you, wanting to be a leader or a manager for the prospects of earning more money and creating a better life for yourself and your family is absolutely an honest reason to want to take on this position within whatever organization you are currently in or planning on going into. I mean, honestly, who would want to do more work with more stress for the same money or less money? That would be crazy and one of the biggest reasons most people to consider being a manager is for the prospect of the immediate pay raise that will come with the position and title. The bonus checks, profit sharing, stock options, extra vacation time, or whatever incentives your company offers all factor in to the overall value of the compensation package offered. To be brutally honest, when I took my first-level leadership position I did it for the extra $1 an hour and double bonus checks I knew I was already doing the work of my then-supervisor anyway, so why not get paid for it? I had no grand plan to move up to an assistant manager or store manager, or district manager and focus on developing people and their skill sets and assets to the company. I was slightly selfish and was just focused on me and how I could earn more money as quickly and easily as possible. This is unfortunately how many of you are probably thinking right now, and while that's ok to admit and accept for a low level-leadership position without much concern. But for career advancement and earning even more money down the road, you must know that to truly become a leader and take full advantage of the financial benefits which can come from being a good leader, you have to know that it's not about you, but about your people and how you cultivate your workforce to be an ever improving team. While that may sound odd for now, let that simmer and we'll come back to that later in the book. For now, let's focus on the question you must now ask yourself, Why Me, Why Now?

Why Me? When I think about the perfect response I would want to hear as the interviewer, I want to hear that they understand that this is a hard position and that they've put a bit of research into what the position entails and that they can speak to things that they have done to set themselves up for success in the position they are seeking. When you think about "why me?", hopefully you have a list of attributes you possess that you can clearly articulate to the interviewer to let them know you are a hard working individual, that you are able to quickly problem solve while working through multiple alternative solutions, that you are able to develop others and have no concerns with delegation and follow up and then accountability if it came to that point, that you understand you are only as strong as your team and that you fully intend to get to know their strengths and weaknesses and put those to action in your business action plans, as well as a laundry list of many other items that you can pick up on by continuing to read the following chapters that will sharpen existing talents and develop new skill sets. I would urge you to write down the list of skill sets you think the position you are in currently or are seeking would require from the most important down to the least important and then rank yourself from 1-5 on a scale of absolutely no clue what I'm doing at 1 to I'm 100% confident in my ability to be the best at 5. Any area in which you rank below a 4 you should stop and work on that skill right away, so you can say you knew it was a potential issue and you took actions to start correcting it before it became an issue. This will better prepare you and show the person interviewing you that you are serious about the position and that you will do whatever it takes to succeed.

Why Now? When I think about "why now?" for me I want to hear that the person has spent enough time in the position they are currently in to learn the basics of the company, the culture, the SOPs, and what is and isn't working from an employee standpoint. (If you are seeking a leadership position at a different place of employment than your current employer you can still use your time in position at your current employer to your advantage of learning market experience) I want to hear that this person has taken their time to understand what is expected of a leader in this position and that they know (not "FEEL", but "KNOW") that they are ready for this new challenge and that they have worked hard to get into consideration and will do whatever it takes when they are finally given the position. I understand you can never truly "know" you are ready before you are in the position, but if you have the confidence in your voice, posture, and facial expressions as you deliver that message and do truly believe that you are ready you will come across well above many of the others seeking the same position as you. I want to hear that this person has spent their time up to this point learning and can tell me that they have worked on their ability to do some of those crucial skill sets you listed out before and can speak to what they specifically have done to show they now currently possess that skill set. For example, let's say you listed out that one of the most crucial skills was delegation and follow-up. You can then tell the interviewer you know one of the most crucial skill sets in this position will be your ability to delegate and follow up. You can then tell them how in your current position even though you don't have the official title of supervisor or manager that you have taken ownership of a specific area of the business and have been delegating worklists, tasks, or assignments. Then show that you followed up with those employees to see how the tasks were completed and the results. When you can say that your peers are already respecting you as a leader without the title, and that's what clicked for you personally on the "why me, why now" reason, you know you are going to truly be ready.

As I have sat down with people over the past 15 years I have seen the good, the bad, and the ugly answers from people seeking leadership positions. While in many of them I could see leadership potential, they just did not have the skillsets or mind frame of someone who was truly ready and capable of the position at that time. It was then I knew that I had to do something to help those people get themselves in a better situation and help make their wishes come true to get the chance at one of the leadership positions. As I researched books, websites, and training to recommend to them I found that most if not all of them were geared toward high-level leadership and assume you already have most of the required skill sets, focused on just one skillset and spread it out over WAY too long of a book, or were just a bunch of words on pages that were written in hypothetical theory and not by someone who has worked as a retail employee and then leader, let alone someone who has lived and breathed more than $750,000,000 in retail sales, such as myself! I know that the following chapters will help you to learn how to separate yourself from the pack, increase your skills, and set yourself up to succeed in an expedited manner versus having to learn as you go and make up solutions for problems you didn't even know existed. The great thing about how I wrote this book is that you don't have to read it from start to finish to get the full value of the information. You can skip around chapter by chapter to focus on what you think are your greatest opportunities, you can read cover to cover, and you can come back later to a specific chapter to refresh your knowledge and skills if something new presents itself as you become a leader. I honestly wish this book would have been available to me when I first started and am happy to now be able to share this knowledge with anyone looking to better their lives via their retail leadership careers. I wish you all the best in your career endeavors and hope that if this book does help you that you share its knowledge with others you know are in your same situation now. Let's get started....

Chapter Two
What People Want in a Leader

While most leaders think about and understand what they want from their employees most leaders don't step back and think about what their employees want from them. As a leader it is your responsibility to ensure that your employees are comfortable with you as a leader if you want to truly get their buy-in and dedication to the job because "they don't want to let you down" more than "they don't want to get in trouble". A paraphrased funny quote that would tie into this is from the show *The Office* where Michael Scott says "Do I want my people to fear me or love me? Both, I want them to be afraid how much they love me." While this cannot always be the case and each employee is going to want something slightly different from their leader than their peers, there are a few common things that many employees would like to see in anyone they report to in a leadership role.

Here are some of the characteristics and leadership qualities that can make for you being a leader your employees would want to work for:

- You are first and foremost a "leader" and not a "manager". You do not micromanage the day-to -day tasks and trust and empower your people to do their jobs effectively because you have trained them to have the ability to do so. You support them in decisions whenever possible and don't try to tell them how you would have done it, even if you would have done it differently.
- You respect your employees and earn their respect as a result. You treat each individual with dignity and never as "just an employee".

- You are approachable at work and never show negative emotions in front of broad groups. You are aware of how your attitude and behavior affects those around you, and you truly care about having a positive and open environment at work.

- You are an active listener. You pay attention to the individual in front of you and can turn off outside distractions when doing so. You make the time to talk whenever someone needs to right away and not push it off till later.

- You are clear and concise in your messages and processes and don't change direction often and on a whim so those around you can be easily aware of what you want and how you want it.

- You value diversity and inclusion and understand that each individual on your team has intrinsic value based on their past experiences. You look to take the opportunity to recognize and allow these employees to showcase their individual talents and skill sets whenever possible.

- You value your team's engagement and input and allow them to have a voice without fear of reprisal if they have an idea to improve efficiency, process, structure, etc. You truly give your sales associates a voice.

- You don't "judge a fish by how well it can climb a tree". You understand that as a leader it is your responsibility to put the right people in the right positions and allow them to succeed. If you determine someone has value but is just in the wrong placement you take actions to help that individual have a chance to succeed by moving them to the right fit for you both.

- When you have criticism or potentially negative feedback to offer, you give it immediately and in private; never in front of others. You give specific details and you have a two-way conversation and then offer suggestions and support to improve every time.

- When you have positive feedback and recognition to provide you do so promptly and in public, so others can hear and make it a bigger deal. You give specific details so that the employee being recognized as well as peers around know what they did and can work to do it again.

- You are open to and, in fact, welcome feedback on your style and approach and don't take it personal if feedback is not always positive. You are humble enough to admit when you don't know the answer or when you've made a mistake. You are willing to learn from the people around you regardless of status and never try to be the smartest person in the room.

- You do not believe "the customer is always right". You may bend and break for the sake of a customer satisfaction situation, but you will never do so at the expense of an employee. You will support your employees and even if you override a decision you will validate that the employee was correct in what they said and did and thank them for doing so. (That is unless they were egregiously wrong in the way they were handling a situation)

- You have created a culture of giving positive recognition when it is deserved. You are not only engaging with the top talent or the most vocal employees but engaging with all levels of talent and tenure in the company that report to you.

- You are decisive and never wishy-washy. You stick to your decisions and do not go back on them without ample time to allow for success or failure. You are not afraid to make a decision and do not have a fear of failure.

- You are aware of how other leaders in the business treat their employees and hold them to the same standards you have for yourself. You do not allow other leaders to create a workplace that is inconsistent with your vision and direction.

- You expect that all leaders and employees in your business treat each other as well as your customers with respect and dignity. You will not stand for inappropriate behavior and will take action immediately if needed.

- You're aware of your body language and facial expressions when speaking to your employees and try to present an open and welcoming persona.

- You use your position as a leader to help develop your people's potential for advancement over and above your own advancement. You understand that it is not about you, but it is about your people.

- You don't accept substandard performance or efforts. You give your best attempt to coach and redirect people who aren't a positive influence in the business and if they cannot do so they are removed from the company. You are honest and upfront with these individuals and don't fear accountability.

- You actively seek to know who your employees are on a personal basis and what motivates them as a person and not just as part of the team. You value spending time with individuals weekly to engage in something other than a work to-do list.

These are just a few characteristics and leadership qualities. However, it should get you a good jump start on things that you can be aware of to work on being someone your people "want to" work for and not "have to" work for. If you are aware and able to adapt these into your daily work experiences, then you will be heads and tails above the average leader in your position.

As a leader it is your responsibility to understand what your people expect and value in a leader and as much as possible you must work to adapt to them and not expect them to adapt to you. I was once told when promoted to a new store manager role that I was entering "their store" and not "my store," and I would know when I earned the right to call it my store because the employees would let me know. Until then, it was their store and I was an outsider trying to break in and become part of their team rather than immediately asking them to become part of my team. Please look to add your own list of things you would want from your leader and then sit back and reflect on whether you are currently emulating those same characteristics. Reading over this list and chapters in this book as I wrote it I reminded myself daily on things that I know better but didn't always execute fully and I would then refocus and try to get better every day for my people.

Chapter Three
Meeting Your Team /
Assessing talent

(Don't judge a fish by how well it can climb a tree)

The first thing you need to do when you finally get that promotion whether you are now a supervisor, and assistant manager, a key holder, a store manager, or even a district manager is to meet your team and assess their individual talents. Understand that as you are meeting and assessing your team they too will be judging you and your skill sets, so you want to be prepared for first interactions and the coming days and weeks that follow with a plan to make sure you and each of your employees have a strong working relationship built on a solid foundation. If you aren't careful, you can build a shaky foundation and make your life an awful lot more difficult than it needs to be, especially when you are just starting out in a new position. This is even more crucial if you are going into a new environment where you do not personally know any of the current employees and they do not know you. If you already know the people and maybe came from within the company or location this step still makes sense to pay close attention to as they will now have to "meet" you as a leader instead of a peer. If the boundaries aren't set correctly they will try to take advantage of that, more often than not.

When you first meet your team, your focus should be to learn about them on a personal level and not talk about the business as much as possible. I like to think of the first week or so as an extended meet-and-greet session where I'm walking around shaking hands and stopping to take the time to engage with and speak to my new employees one on one without any other agenda. This will feel a bit weird at first as I'm sure you are thinking that by not taking a bunch of actions and giving direction to set expectations during your first week you will come off as weak or too easy on them. But, again, remember you are looking to build a relationship, so they know they can trust you and you have their best interests at heart versus just yours or the best interest of the business. I would suggest you do a light prep before you initiate these interactions such as a complete employee listing with full names, job titles, tenure in position and, in the best-case scenario, a few notes on each of them or at least the top performers so you are not going in fully blind. If another leader who was already in place is still there I would get that information from them and then ask them to walk through the building with you as you start your introductions. This way, they can remind you of important employees as you meet them.

Topics to bring up during these meetings are slightly business related, but not too intrusive, and then a few minor personal questions that may dig deeper depending on their responses and comfort level with how the conversation is going. I like to start with a friendly greeting along with a smile and a handshake and introduce myself first as the new leader (insert title here for whatever you call it, Store Manager, General Manager, Assistant Manager, Night Manager, Department Supervisor, Team Lead, etc.). I like to get their name and what their specific role is as early as possible, and generally do so by asking something along the lines of "What is it you do here?" Once I give them a chance to answer, I like to follow up with "How long have you been doing that?" "How is that going for you?" First things first. If they have been there for more than a year, please make sure that you thank them for their dedication to the location and let them know that you value them for doing so. I like to say something along the lines of "That's awesome! I'm glad to hear everything has been going well for you here," if their answer was positive. If you find a hint of anything negative in the reply I would follow up with something more along the lines of, "That's awesome! Might I ask why? 'This gives them the option to tell you if anything had been on their chest for career goals, maybe problems with previous leadership that they are concerned about happening again, etc. I would then move into a very low confrontational personal question such as "What is it that you like to do for fun?" I like this one as it could open to a common hobby or interest that you can build a bond over. Maybe they tell you that they are a big family-oriented person and you can then tell them about your family to make yourself more "human" to them. Maybe they tell you that they are a homebody and like to just veg on the couch and watch TV. Whatever their response is, please find a way to relate to it and show a form of interest. Once you know what that is I would also suggest that you have a journal or notepad of some kind whether paper or electronic that you can record what was discussed. This will allow you to access that information later to remind yourself when you next need to engage with them again, whether in a positive or negative manner. To this day, I find simple things such as knowing a person is a huge baseball fan and if I saw their team was on a hot streak taking the time to stop by to congratulate them. You would be surprised how they light up that you remember, and that they get to talk to you for a few minutes about something other than a work-related task. I assure you this employee will be much more open to your direction and feedback because you have proven that you care about them and were not just faking it as you met the first time.

When given the opportunity for having the information up front on who some of your top sales people are, top operations people, top whatever position, please make note of them prior to your first conversation. I like to take that first interaction as a chance to validate to that employee that their hard work and great results had not gone unnoticed, and just because there is a new leader in the building that they won't have to work their way back up to the top of the list for recognition, etc. Imagine the relief of these top employees when you can walk up and greet them and then throw out a personal thank you for being one of the top performers. I like to say something along the lines of "I've heard a lot about you and your contributions over the last year/month(s) and I wanted to personally thank you for what you've done to help this location be successful. It's good to know we have someone I can count on if I have any questions while I'm learning the ropes around here." This gives them some personal validation that they know they are already being recognized as a top performer for what they had done before you arrived as well as you looking to them as a trusted and valued asset in the building if you needed assistance.

When you are meeting the first time I would caution giving almost any form of direction or feedback other than a resounding positive commendation on feedback you have seen or heard. Imagine meeting your new leader and they walk up to you and one of the first sentences they speak to you is about picking up trash off the floor, or selling more, or commenting on dress code, or whatever minor thing they thought made sense to give direction to at the time. You would feel more than likely disrespected and that you don't need someone telling you to pick up the garbage or sweep because that's something you do later in your shift, and why are they assuming that you were ignoring it? A lot of stupid thoughts run through people's heads and they generally read more into them. When it happens on a first interaction they now feel they must overcome a bad first impression and build up to earn your respect. So, again, at all costs--no matter how minor you think it is--do NOT give direction on your first meeting. Wait at a minimum until the second meeting when you can start "asking" them to do things for you.

Now that you have met your team and have a basic understanding of who works where and what they are accountable for you must move on to making your own assessment of them individually based off their current contributions and efforts. I cannot count the number of times I have come into a new building and been told that so-and-so is a piece of garbage to then find out that they once were a top performer and had since gone unrecognized so they fell off of their game because they believed that no one cared about who they were and what they could do because they were treated the same as their average peer. The problem with treating everyone as an average employee is eventually they will all fall into the performance of an "average" employee and stop striving to be at the top, where they can and should be treated better via recognition, compensation, development, etc.

A common complaint from many managers is that they have a team of individuals with no talent and that's why they struggle to perform at a higher level. I, too, have fallen into this trap complaining that a store I just took over as the new store manager had a team of leaders with limited leadership skills and no one trained and ready to go to replace them if I wanted to make moves. I was blaming previous leadership for their poor decisions on who they had placed in the leadership roles and complaining about why they hadn't been training anyone else below them to build a bench of talent to always have someone ready to go to replace an open leadership position. The problem with this situation is it is a self-fulfilling prophecy. If you believe you have no one worthy of doing the task at hand or delivering the result needed, then you will eventually fail. What many forget to do is judge people by their abilities and not by your own standard of perfection. I like to use the old saying of not judging a fish by how well it can climb a tree. If you haven't heard that one before it is basically a metaphor quoting Albert Einstein for setting someone up to fail and then being upset that they did indeed fail. If you had a monkey and a fish and you told the fish to climb a tree and the monkey to swim across the lake what do you think is going to happen? The fish is sure not going to be able to climb that tree and no matter how much motivation and direction you give that fish it was just not meant to do that task and as a result will fail and feel defeated in their ability to do the next task. The monkey, on the other hand, may be able to tread water and get across that lake but sure won't do it as efficiently and fast as the fish. As a result, at the end you are mad at the monkey for being too slow and not able their task done on time. What you need to take from this silly analogy is that maybe the people you were told suck or are no good are simply being utilized for the wrong position or task, and if they were put somewhere they could excel and shine they could turn into a valued asset. You, as the leader, are responsible to take the poor performance at face value and determine if it is because of not knowing how to do the job or not caring, or in some instances not being competent or capable.

I have a real-life example of a current assistant manager who would fall into this discussion perfectly. A long time ago when I was this employee's supervisor and they were just an hourly employee they were seen as a hard worker and a get-it-done guy, but never as a leader. When discussions were had about this employee wanting to become a supervisor the conversation quickly went to the fact that he was a great worker but not a great leader and that he would fail if we put him in that spot. He was not he not even going to be given the chance. I had to break the news to him that he was not going to be considered for the position and that it was because he wasn't seen as having the ability to be a leader versus a worker. This frustrated him to the point that he did not put forth the full efforts in his current role as he didn't want to be seen as "just a hard worker" anymore and if his efforts weren't going to yield results, then why keep performing at a high level? I had to sit him down and document him to the point that he was on the verge of termination if he didn't change his attitude and mentality of the situation. When we were game planning for how to get better this was an aha moment for me that if we treated him like "just a hard worker" then he would never be more than that. We were setting him up to fail if we did give him that role as we had never spent the time to tell him what to work on and how to get there. I promised to help him start working on some leadership skills and told him that he had to get back to his old habits of being a top performer, but add the ability to lead his peers on top of that, to engage with the assistant managers and store manager to show them what he was doing and why it made sense for the business, and how he was involving others in getting it done versus doing it all himself. Because of this, within a year he was promoted to supervisor and is now a strong assistant manager at a different location where he can teach his people both the ability to get stuff done as well as how to get it done through leadership and his people. Had we let labels or predetermined judgement keep him stuck in that bad spot he would have been gone from the company and had a sour note in his thoughts on us as an organization. Because leadership stopped to assess his true abilities, instead I was able to get his perceptions changed and move him into a position in which he could use his skills to achieve success.

As you assess your team's talents please make sure to stop to think whether they are in the right position for them to feel the most comfortable and deliver the best results. Are they in a sales role and should really be in a labor role, or are they in a labor role but have a great personality and should really be in a customer service role, or are they struggling on the late shift because they are a morning person and they lose physical motivation after a certain point in the day? These are just a few of the infinite examples of how someone could be seen as a lost cause or a bad employee but as a result of us putting them into that position and not listening to them when they tell us either directly via conversations initiated as a result of their performance or indirectly via their actions that they would be better fit and an asset versus a liability in a different role.

Now, I'm not saying everyone who is an underperformer will be able to be fixed. There will be certain people who fall into the bad-apple category who are not good performers and it is not because of placement or competency but because of their drive and performance. These people need to be treated just as the others where you meet and assess their talents and abilities and attempt to correct their placement or training. If it is still determined that this person is more of a liability than an asset to you, then you should move on and proceed down the path for termination before they affect the morale and performance of your overall environment and team any further.

Chapter Four
Managing by Exception

The concept of managing by exception can be used anywhere that you have top and bottom performers as well as a majority who will make up the middle and are just average. When working in small groups and smaller numbers it is better to engage with each associate one on one. This way you can provide personal feedback and accountability or recognition but when you just don't have the time in your week to hit every person. This technique will save you time and still ensure that the people who truly need your attention the most will receive it.

You only have so much time in a day and I'm guessing are (or will be) working 10-12 hours a day already, so every minute you can save to focus on other items that require your attention is invaluable! What if I told you that you could speak to just 20-40% of your workforce and see improved results from all ends of your staff spectrum? I know it sounds too good to be true, but just trust the process and follow the steps and you too will see the benefits in your staff's productivity.

Think of your team right now and a metric that you know is important that is easily tracked and equally important to your business. I am sure if you put pen to paper you could easily rank these associates from top to bottom. For this example, we'll assume it's 10 people you are tracking, however, this same technique could just as easily be used with 20, 30, or even 100+ employees. At the top you are going to have 2-3 employees who are driving the bulk of your results (sales, credit, leads, contracts, etc.) and who you would probably not have made your expected plan without their contributions. This is the "Top" 10-20%. At the bottom you are going to have 2-3 associates who are dragging down your numbers and average (even if they are still achieving their goal numbers), this is the "Bottom" 10-20%. In the middle you are going to have your "average" performers who are producing results but not shooting to be at the top and generally want to stay off the radar of being on the bottom as well.

I want you to take a minute to go ahead and jot down these names. Then let's run through this exercise together. For the sake of this exercise all I want you to write down are the names and results of the "top" performers and the "bottom" performers and their results. Ignore the average "middle" performers all together. The top and bottom performers are now effectively the "exceptions" and are standouts from the average performers on your team. You should use 10-20% as a guide to determine the number for the top- and bottom-performer list that you should use for this exercise. You can expand or contract this number on future exercises.

First, let's start with the top performers who are generally going to be at the top of this list each week/month/quarter for whatever time frame you choose to use for the exercise and are very valuable and important to the success of your organization. Imagine what would happen if these associates were no longer with you and you had to drop them off your list or if they dropped down into the middle of your list where their results are now just average. That is a very scary thought but is what could and will happen if these associates aren't recognized and then challenged to deliver on those results again. The analogy of water will always flow through the path of least resistance definitely applies here and you cannot afford for these associates to ever feel neglected or that their contributions are going unnoticed or unvalued. You want to make sure you budget the time early in your week (preferably the first shift of that associate) to walk up to them and thank them in person for their results, go over those results in detail i.e.:

"Bob, I just wanted to personally thank you for the sales you delivered last week! Did you know that not only were you the number one sales associate on the team last week, but your numbers helped the team make their goal and we might not have made it without you? Anything you are doing that I can share with your peers to help them deliver similar results? Either way I just wanted to take the time to thank you again and I look forward to seeing what you can do again this week, I'm counting on you!"

How do you think this associate feels now that the manager has come to them personally to thank them for what they did? Do you think they will work even harder this week now that the manager has specifically asked them personally to deliver on the same results again? I can assure you, if done right, this associate will not only achieve similar results, if not better, but they will be looking for you first thing next week to come brag about their results since your last conversation! Whenever possible you want to have these conversations in areas where other employees that are probably in the middle or bottom can hear the recognition and hopefully motivate them to step up their game, so they can get some of that recognition. A verbal or physical thank you and high five or handshake can go an awful lot further than a bonus or formal recognition with these employees. Follow these same steps and make sure to get through your top performer list ASAP each week.

Next will come the bottom performers. While a lot of people like to shy away from these associates because of the uncomfortable conversations, if you don't have them you are effectively accepting their results and telling them they can continue to underperform without fear of reprimand. This is not only a bad business practice if you don't have the conversation but can demoralize the employees at the top of the list and even the middle of the list as to why they should even try to perform higher and get to the top. Think about it. If you knew another manager was getting the same pay but working less, delivering lower results, and was still employed and not being held accountable how would that make you feel? I'd be pissed and, I assure you, employees who are not as highly compensated as you will be a lot less forgiving to the lack of accountability to their peers.

The process flows the same as your top performer list where you write down their names and results and where they rank on your team. The bottom performers are generally going to be at the bottom of this list each week/month/quarter as well and are very detrimental to the success of your organization. Imagine what would happen if these associates were no longer with you and you were able to drop them off your list or if they, better yet, rose up into the middle of your list where their results are now at least "average". Yes, I know even if these associates rise up and deliver there will still be a bottom performer list and it could even be these same employees. But wouldn't you rather have a higher-performing bottom performer list than the one you have now? What would the increase in results mean to your organization if these employees were able to raise their performance on a regular basis? The numbers can be staggering. You cannot afford for these employees to ever feel like they can fly under the radar and that their contributions are going unnoticed. You want to make sure that you budget the time early in your week (again, preferably the first shift of that associate) to call them back to your office to have this conversation in private i.e.:

"Bob, I just wanted to personally discuss the sales you delivered these last month. How do you think you did this last month? Did you know that you were one of the lowest-performing sales associates on the team last month? I just wanted to take the time to make sure you were aware and wanted to see what I can do to help you deliver better results starting this week?"

You must be sincere in this conversation and not use it as a beat-up session or a "Come to Jesus" meeting, but rather a meeting where they have a chance to be heard and they feel like you truly care about their success. Try to use some of your own feedback or maybe even feedback from a peer in one of your top-performer meetings as to things they can implement to improve their own results.

How do you think this associate feels now that the manager has come to them personally to discuss tier results? Do you think they will work even harder this week now that the manager has specifically asked them personally to deliver better results? I can assure you, if done right, this associate will not only achieve better results, but they will be looking for you first thing next week to come brag about their improved results since your last conversation! You must make small checkpoints with this associate after this conversation to keep them on their toes and give them recognition for small milestone wins on their way to coming off that bottom-performer list. A verbal or physical thank you and high five or handshake can also go an awful lot further than a bonus or formal recognition with these employees as well. Follow these same steps and make sure to get through your bottom performer list asap each week.

Lastly, as far as the middle of the list, I am going to tell you to technically ignore it for the sake of follow-up purposes but keep it handy as you will hopefully start seeing some of these employees coming to you after hearing recognition you have delivered to their peers and wanting to know how they are doing. They likely will have heard that some of the employees were back in your office going over their results. You want to use these interactions to motivate these employees to try to get to the top of the list as well as to stay off the bottom. You will find some hidden gems on your team through these conversations and you need to add them to your follow-up list for at least the next week or two after they speak to you to keep their interest alive.

When you follow this process if you will keep the top of the list happy and they will deliver even better results, you will keep the bottom of the list on their toes and will be easily able to determine who needs coaching and who needs accountability and possibly removed from your team, and your middle of the road performers will continue to chug along delivering consistent albeit average results. When it comes review time this will also make their performance evaluations go smoother and you won't have any surprised employees wondering why they are being rated poorly if it comes to that. All this will also free up more time for you to spend on other pressing matters that you need to get completed. I hope you find the value in this and start to use it immediately in your environment asap!

Just for fun let me throw out an example of when I used this to turn around some negative results in one of my stores. At my store we heavily tracked customer service levels via a survey at the bottom of the receipt that was then to be filled out by the consumer at home. You would hope that your employees had delivered great enough service that the customers would go home and give you great scores that would then reflect in your weekly result. Unfortunately, most customers even if happy are not willing to go onto the website to complete the survey unless they were on either end of the completely satisfied or completely dissatisfied spectrum. We went a few weeks where our customer service numbers were slightly below where we wanted to be ranging from 80%-85% and I trusted my operations manager and front-end supervisor over the cashiers to fix the result and bring it up above the goal that was set at 90% completely satisfied. The problem with this was that we were not making up any ground after three weeks and when I asked them to now detail out to me their plans on how they were going to fix it they said "Well, we have told everyone the goal so I'm not sure why it's not improving". Knowing that this strategy would not get us to where we needed to be I asked them both to grab the cashier reporting by employee and meet me in my office. When we sat down I had them count the total number of employees who had rung up transactions, the total number of transactions (opportunities for surveys), and then list out the top 5 and bottom 5. Once they had completed this I asked them one by one if they had spoken to the top 5 cashiers and if they had thanked them for their solid results and if they had asked them how they were able to achieve better results than the rest, so they could share it with the ones struggling. Obviously, the answer was "no" or a quick "Well, I told them 'good job,' but that was it". When I then asked if they had done one-on-ones with the bottom performers who, if were making their results would have brought up the entire stores average to where we would have made goal, the answer again was a resounding "no" or "not yet." At this point I could not trust that they would achieve any better results on their own, so I said that I was going to start having weekly meetings with the bottom performers in my office each week and that every Monday I wanted them to bring me the list of top 10 and bottom 10 so I could make them happen. Side note: (Making them complete the list for me helped them build a routine weekly for themselves). The first step was to go out to the front end with them both and start the recognition process for the top 10! We went out as a group and went right up to our No. 1 performing cashier and the conversation went as follows: I greeted her and asked how her day was going and how the traffic had been so far that day. Then

I asked a few questions on what our company goal was for the survey (which she knew), and then if she knew what the store was currently performing at and if we were missing or making it (which she did not know). Then I asked her if she knew what her score was (which she did not, Yikes!). At this point I brought up the energy and gave her a high five as I told her that not only was she exceeding our company goal and our store's average, but she was our No. 1 performing cashier in the entire store and I wanted to thank her for her contributions! She was blown away that the entire leadership team above her was there to recognize her for doing a great job, as well as doing it out in front of other employees and customers, which made her feel even better! Before we left the area, I asked her to tell me her secret on how she was doing it and her answer "I just treat customers with respect and I ask every customer to complete the survey when I finish up; that's it". I told her that if it's that simple then just keep it up and she'll stay No. 1! I then took the operations manager and supervisor back to my office to discuss the interaction we just had and ask them if I did anything they could not replicate which they both agreed they could. I then challenged them to go through the rest of the top 10 before I found them, so they were aware of their goals, the store results, etc., unlike the first one, and to make that a habit each week going forward. At this point I asked them to leave my office, so I could call back the bottom cashier who was there to have a one-on-one in my office. As the cashier showed up to the office she was visibly nervous as most employees would be with a manager calling them back to the office to speak. I asked her to come in and have a seat and not to be worried, "You're not in trouble, I just want to talk to you about some of your cashier metrics."

When she sat down we had the exact same conversation as with the top cashier whether she knew the goal, did she know our overall result, did she know her personal result, etc. As far as the personal result for her, I gave her her number of just 65% satisfied and asked her why she thought that she would be rated so low and then what she was doing to drive this result. First, she was not aware of her result and was honestly surprised that she was a bottom performer and wished someone had said something to her before I had. I then asked her to tell me what she was doing to drive the survey results up as at this point because based on the math said she had to get 10 perfect 100% scores to raise her number back to above a 90%. She was at a loss for what to do and so I kept it simple and told her all I wanted her to do was be the most friendly cashier she could be and when it came time to talk about the survey to let the customers know that she was personally rated on this survey and that she needs to get 10 by the end of the month and that she would really appreciate it if they could go on and let us know how she was doing. I told her that she needs to make it personal and not just another "store" survey but a personal cashier survey about her. I told her at that point that I was going to meet with a few more of the lower performing cashiers and that the next week I would be doing the same and I hoped that she would not be on that list the next week which she at that point assured me she would not, now that she knew some tips and tricks on how to get better results. She left the room feeling good about the conversation but also understanding that she had better go out and deliver some results. I proceeded with this same conversation with the rest of the bottom 5 all within the next two days so they had plenty of time in the week to affect their results and all the conversations went very much the same as the first.

Come Monday, when the report came out, we had made the jump from 86% the last week to 91% this week! The supervisor who brought me the report out for the top and bottom performers was super pumped up about the jump as well and said she had already met with the top 2 before she even brought me the report and had it marked on her schedule to meet with the bottom 2 who were in later that day as well. I told her that I was going to keep meeting with the top and bottom and I appreciated her support in doing the same and asked her to keep it up! The next week we rose to 94%, then 95% and held steady above 90% for the rest of the quarter with this simple process of recognition for top performers and personal accountability for the bottom performers! The list of bottom performers after a month got to the point where there were only 1-2 below the 90% goal and they were well aware and were coming to me at that point to let me know they would be back on top next week and to just watch! We built a sustainable model for follow up, built weekly habits and routines for my leaders, and improved our scores to best in class in our district at the same time, all while only spending the bulk of follow-up time with 15-20% of the associates who drove the most important metrics!

I turned over these meetings to the front-end manager and the operations manager after the first few weeks so they could take personal ownership of the process and so they could feel more engaged in the positive outcome trends that were being delivered. This was a win for us both as I set them up for being able to come back and recap great results. As a direct result of their follow through on the process I had helped them become better leaders versus me doing it and them feeling out of the loop. Had I to do this process again I would have had them sit in with me on the first meetings and turn them over to them completely for the following meetings and not wait the few weeks that I did to do them myself and feel overly confident that we were making the improvements needed. I set a process in place and helped them deliver a win with only having to spend time focusing on the top and bottom performers and getting back to other priorities. I hope that you can replicate this example in your business and build your own sustainable follow up and recognition/redirection process.

Chapter Five
A Day in the Life of a Leader...
(It's not about you)

So, you're now a member of management, now what? A lot of managers see themselves as the most important person in the organization and expect that they are no longer going to have to "work," that people immediately owe them respect, and that they have arrived! Let me be the first to burst that bubble and tell you that while decisions you make are extremely important and the processes you put in place can make or break your organization, but you need to know that ultimately you aren't magically special, and you aren't owed a thing by anyone!

Your role as a manager will change daily and is a fluid position which is one of the things that I enjoy most about being a manager. As a manager, you need to adapt to the environment and not expect the environment and employees to adapt to you. As noted in a previous chapter, I was once told that when I enter the store as a new manager that it is the employees store and not mine and if I treat it that way I will succeed and that if I treated it as mine from day one that the employees would lose respect and make my life a whole lot harder. That advice helped me overcome initial hurdles that I have seen other managers step into and fail time and time again by letting their ego and title get in the way of their actual role. Effectively, if you strip down your role as a manager there are some basic key roles and responsibilities you need to execute and the rest of your time can be spent doing the fun parts of the job whether that be interacting with employees or customers on the sales floor, strategizing new ideas for sales or productivity, reading reports, or whatever else floats your boat.

The first and most basic function of a manager is to manage, or better yet, to lead. You will manage employees, you will manage productivity, you will manage hiring and firing, you will manage customer complaints and satisfaction, you will manage payroll, you will manage expenses, you will manage sales goals, you will manage inventory levels, and you will manage other managers potentially, among 100's of other things you will "manage" day to day. A great manager will be able to differentiate what truly needs to be "managed" and what they should do as a "leader." The concept of being a manager versus being a leader is not new and should hopefully not be a foreign concept to you at this point in your career. I was once told "It's not about you anymore." It's about your people and what they need, what your customers need, what you can do for them versus what they can do for you. Let that sink in for a second as I'm sure that's backwards thinking from what you have been brought up to know as a manager. At the end of the day you are replaceable if you don't bring value to the company just as the manager you replaced to earn your current position or the position you are looking to fulfill! How does a manager bring value to the organization? They do it through their people and they surround themselves with and bring talented people along with them on their path to success!

As a manager you "manage" things, which can be great for things that are black and white such as controlling expenses, hitting operating costs budget, exceeding profit margins, increasing productivity, etc. Anyone can manage a metric when they are given a goal to hit. That is the easy part. Becoming a "Leader" is a whole other animal.

As a "leader" you lead people and are seen as part of the team versus being a manager who is "better than them." You involve them in making decisions, so they have good input versus simply telling them your final decision. You work side by side as you roll out new processes to see the effectiveness hands on and get real-life feedback from your employees on what is and isn't working. You stand up for failures and take ownership versus placing the blame on the employees by a manager who would say they "just didn't get it done." These are just a few examples of which there are thousands more where you can be a more effective "manager" in title by actually being a "leader" with your employees.

If you were to think back to people who were your managers and the ones you loved and hated which ones were managers and which ones were leaders? Which ones are you going to look to emulate in your role as a manager? At some point down the road your goal should be to have some of your current employees look to you as who they would name one of the managers who was truly a servant leader that made an impact on their lives and who they would want to emulate as a manager as they move up through the ranks someday. That is how you know you truly made an impact versus just managed the business.

Put simply, when you need to decide on approaching the matter at hand and are unsure whether to approach as a leader or a manager, make sure you understand the differences you just read and take that into account before you move forward with your plan of action.

As an employee looking to move up, before you were promoted everything you did was about "you" as a leader and how what "you" did produced a positive result, how "you" led this project and beat the timeline by 3 weeks, how "you" held your peers accountable to job duties before you had the official title of manager, how "you" were the badass they would be stupid to not promote into the next open position. This is great at that level as you must prove who "you" are at that time and how "you" can influence and direct employees to accomplish what you set forward. Now, though, as you have the official title and have "arrived" as the next great leader in your company, you need to understand it is no longer about "you" and what "you" can do but it is about your "people" who deliver these results and how you can continue to influence them to want to do more. You will have to lose the "me" mentality quickly or your employees will know what's top on your priority list. If it is not them they will know and will perform as such.

I want to dive deeper into the reason you are there as a leader in whatever environment you are in at the time. You are there to lead people, you are there to hire, develop, retain and promote those people, you are there to ensure a positive experience for your customers and ensure that they keep coming back to you for future business, you are there for others and note that everything you are there for is not about you; it's about your people! When you go through the day looking to take credit for success versus going out and recognizing the employee or employees who made that success possible you are thinking about you and not your people and doing it wrong. When you go through and complain that you don't have any talented people to promote and your new hires are turning over too fast versus understanding that you haven't spent the time to develop these employees to promote and you haven't found ways to engage with and retain the new hires, you are thinking about how it affects you and not how you can affect these people and are doing it wrong. When you are spending more time worrying about how you can increase your own paycheck and bonus payout versus thinking about how you can motivate your employees to sell more and find ways to increase their own (which will obviously in turn raise yours) and you let them know how much you want them to get the biggest one possible, then you are again thinking about this the wrong way and need to reevaluate your priorities.

As a leader you are only as strong as the group of individuals you surround yourself with and you will find those employees will work harder and be more dedicated to a leader whom they truly feel has their best interest at heart and is not there to just further their own agenda. A servant leader will always be on the lookout for ways to help their people succeed first and then worry about how they impact themselves second. A servant leader knows it's not about them and that their people make or break their career, that their customers make or break their career, and that they themselves only achieve true success when those around them are put first and helped to find success as the first priority. Ask yourself when was the last time you truly spent time with your top salesperson and found out what they want for their future with the company? When was the last time you gave public praise for sales results to an individual or team and took no credit to your supervisor? When was the last time you "asked" an employee what they were working on first before "telling" them what to do next? When was the last time you put effort into cleaning and improving the breakroom or common space for your employees to show them you care about them and their work environment? These employees will see these things if done on a regular basis and will respond to them with more commitment to you and your leadership and will move mountains when you ask because they know you have their backs. Whatever you do you must be doing it for the right reasons!

Put your employees and your customers first and the success you will find as a servant leader who understands it is not about you anymore will be immense! Try to stop and think as you move forward with your leadership style and ask yourself whether you put your employees and customers first or yourself, and how can you make this about improving their lives versus yours. You will see the difference immediately.

Chapter Six
Dealing with Difficult People

While one of the best things about working retail or sales in general, especially in a leadership role, is the constant change and getting to do something different every day that you work. One thing is always constant, and that is having to deal with difficult people from employees to customers and, even sometimes, your upper leadership. This is in my opinion the hardest part of being a leader and unfortunately will never go away or get easy no matter how long you have been in the position, but you can make it more bearable as you learn how to be prepared for these situations mentally and physically.

First, let's go over why people are generally difficult and help get in a better mindset for when you must deal with them. While this is a horrible and broad-brush statement, the public is not always that smart. Not to say they are ignorant or as in just being not "smart", but they have been brought up in many cases to have unreasonable expectations. Most people have expectations that in any establishment because they are a paying customer that anything they say or do should be welcomed and catered to as well as some others even worse having what we call "retail syndrome." Retail syndrome is where people feel even more aggressive in their ability to treat the workers with disrespect and that you and your people just must deal with it because the customer is always right. Well, as you and I both know, the customer in these situations is rarely "right" and no matter what you try to do to assist them you sometimes feel like you are talking to a 2 year old throwing a tantrum or to a brick wall that just doesn't want to hear what you have to say. These people are more than likely the customer side of the equation that you will be dealing with, but it can come from the employee side as well when dealing with someone who refuses to accept poor performance feedback or constructive criticism, fails to agree that assigned tasks are reasonable, fails to comply with policies and procedures because they don't agree, or wants to argue their side of the matter no matter how wrong they truly are and just cannot recognize it. These people were probably raised that way by their parents, they may range from the participation trophy generation all the way to the "back-in- my-day" generation, they may have seen it on TV or in the movies, or maybe they are just an entitled jerk all on their own. Whatever the reason they are the way they are, there are still ways to help yourself overcome the obstacles they present.

The most important thing to remember when dealing with these difficult people is, believe it or not, they just don't know any better. No amount of explanation or reasoning will change the way they are or the way they act. Sometimes these people will have family members with them whom you can tell are embarrassed by their behavior and may have even tried themselves to help them understand the way they are acting is unreasonable. If they can't get through to them then you sure won't be able to as just some random stranger with a "manager" title. These people all generally do have a few things that help to calm them down and resolve the situations. We will cover a few common ones here.

First things first. Your goal for the outcome of dealing with any angry or difficult customer is for them to be as reasonably happy as possible when they leave with as small of a scene as possible in your business environment. Whenever I am called to go meet with a difficult customer I generally ask my employees to call me from a phone out of earshot of the customer whenever possible so they can give me a quick rundown on what the customer is upset about and if they have offered any sort of solution to the problem so I can at least be semi-prepared for the interaction when I arrive to greet them. This will not always be possible in person but is always possible when dealing with someone over the phone. So, stop and make sure you train your staff to go over this with you before to help the rest of the interaction go as smoothly as possible.

When I then arrive to greet the customer with this information upfront I always approach with a smile and a handshake to introduce myself by name and ask for theirs followed by, "Nice to meet you (Customer Name). How can I help you today?" This is a very non-confrontational greeting and will allow you to build up a bit of rapport with them in that very short greeting interaction. Most people will follow that up with a stern question over whether you are truly a manager and if you are the person that can really help them with their complaint. I always assure them with a smile that absolutely I am, and I am happy to be of whatever assistance possible. I normally will then ask them to follow me to a different area away from our main customer traffic if they are somewhere such as your customer service counter or returns area that would have high visibility to other customers or hold up being able to assist other customers who may be in line behind this customer. I would never ask them to go far, but asking them to do so, if even just a few steps aside so that I "will be able to hear them better" will help them understand that you are going to take the time to hear them out and give them your focus and attention until they have a resolution.

Once you have them where you would like to speak to them aside or in an office with a closed door if on the phone, I always start by pulling out a notepad and a pen to take quick notes as they speak. I cannot tell you how many times I have seen other managers get destroyed by an angry customer who had to repeat themselves a second or, god forbid, a third time so I always take notes even if a minor issue. I may have to follow up on it later and get back to this customer with an answer later and you do not want to have to ask them to clarify anything for you again. Even minor details can help you later whether for follow-up with the customer or follow-up with your employee or vendor as needed sometimes.

As you allow them to vent, regardless of the situation, just take the notes quietly and do not respond until they have stopped speaking completely or they ask you to. If you interject with any amount of feedback or response other than maybe in extreme cases with a question to clarify what they said, they will hate you for doing so and will probably accuse you of interrupting them and not listening or caring. So, stop yourself from speaking at all costs and just take the notes at this point. Remain calm and nod as they speak to confirm to them that you understand what they are saying and are getting it as you take notes. Make sure you maintain eye contact whenever you are not taking notes.

The thing that most customers what in these situations is to vent and just make sure someone has heard them and how "wronged" they were by your business, product, employee, or whatever the complaint is. Always allow them to vent and never ever ask them to "calm down." If needed, you can politely ask them to lower their voice, so you can understand them better, but that's only if they are truly causing a scene and yelling. Never listen with the intent to respond; listen with the intent to make sure they understand you have heard them and understand why they are so angry, even if you think it is unreasonable or a trivial concern. Once you have heard them out, taken notes, and let them vent, most customers will calm down a bit at this point and ready to see how you will respond. I always respond with an apology for their situation and thank them for bringing it to my attention because, "If it wasn't brought to my attention I wouldn't have known it was a problem and wouldn't have been able to address it." I then generally try to respond with a recap of what happened to clarify that I truly understood what the problem was. I never try to come up with a response right away or, again, they will think you are just trying to respond versus listening to them and understanding their problem.

After you have heard their complaints and allowed them to vent and have thanked them for bringing it to your attention and used your notes to recap the key points of what happened now you need to come up with some form of reply. I always try to reply with an answer that is firm but vague enough as it is being said in front of other employees and customers. You do not want to admit fault, blame an employee, or worse, blame them for the mistake or problem that was caused—

even if because of their own error—right off the bat, at least. I also never offer a discount or refund right away as they think you are just trying to bribe them with money to make the problem go away. That is never a good solution. Plus, why would you ever want to willingly offer up money back or a discount when it is not necessary? If it were a complaint on a specific person I would assure them I would follow up with this person one on one in the back to make sure they understood the customer's complaint and to see how we can do better in the future so no other customers feel the same way. Notice how I never admitted fault or agreed to reprimand the employee, but I did agree to meet with that employee and make sure they understood the complaint so no one else would feel the same way. Even if I did agree my person was at fault I would not want to say it out in the open for others to hear. That is a conversation that would need to be had one-on-one in private. I would then again thank them for the feedback and ask if there was anything else that I could do for them today. Most customers are fine at this point and will thank you for listening and leave as happy as possible. There will be a few, however, who will ask for a follow-up call regarding how you handle the employee or ask you straight out if you are going to write up or fire that employee. I always respond to this question directly and confidently that, unfortunately, I am not able to disclose what happens from that point for legal reasons. But I could assure them that their concern would not go unheard and that I would take appropriate actions. This, again, isn't always enough but most individuals will accept this as a response and again leave as happy as you could have hoped.

There will be a subset of those difficult people who are fishing for a discount or a refund. How you respond to that is up to you. I would generally handle the situation as stated above and go for just being heard and agreeing to take actions as my answer and let them ask for the discount if they want. But, again, I would never offer it on my side. If they ask you for compensation for the hassle or issue and you decide that you think that it makes sense, then how much is truly up to you to determine based off how bad the situation truly was. I normally like to let them know in that situation that we do not normally offer a discount or compensation depending on how they asked, and I would then ask them what they think is fair resolution. This is a great way to allow them to make the first offer and see how unreasonable they are with their expectations. If they come back and ask for a full refund on a used product or a huge discount on something they want to buy you know that they are not going to be happy with anything other than agreeing to what they ask for, even if you were to offer to meet them in the middle, should you think that was fair. If they come back to you with a reasonable number and you agree to it then I would still make sure they knew it was "not normal" and that you would be able to honor it this one time. Many times, I will still try to meet these customers in the middle or offer a smaller discount or compensation that I felt was fair knowing nothing would satisfy them anyway. I don't cave completely if they were at fault for a portion of the problem. I would also challenge you to think about the value of the discount they are seeking, as it is not worth your time to argue over a tiny amount in the long run of things versus if they are asking for hundreds or thousands. I once had someone chew my ear off for 10 minutes to then ask for a $5 discount. I agreed even though they were a completely crazy customer because it was not worth the argument over $5 to sit there for another 10 minutes.

There will be times where no matter what you do or say nothing will get through to this customer regardless of how nice you were to them and how you listened to everything they said that the outcome they seek is just plain unreasonable. I once had a customer (husband and wife) who signed up for approximately $30,000 in purchases for their home. The husband then flew back to Canada and the wife stayed here and added an additional $20,000 in work to the home that was completed and installed before the husband returned to the states to view the work completed. We did not know that he was out of country or that he was not happy with the pricing because the wife had come in to make the purchases and had the credit card with her name on it, so we proceeded with all purchases as if she was the decision maker, why would we have any reason to think otherwise? When he came back and saw all the extra work and the bills associated with it he came into the store and demanded that we refund the $20,000 right away because "she is a woman and doesn't have the right to approve those purchases!" There was no amount of explaining to this customer that she had authorized the purchases and swiped the credit card and that yes, she did have the right to make purchases with her credit card. In the end we ended up with him leaving threatening to sue us and me asking him not to return to the store unless there were any problems with the work that was completed in his home. I ended up effectively firing this customer as a future customer but that was the best thing that could have happened for both sides. I never did see a lawsuit for that customer as I'm sure the lawyer explained to him that she was the cardholder and had signed off on all purchases and completion contracts and that there was no recourse in that situation for anything done wrong. I'm sure he was then as unreasonable with that lawyer who he disagreed with and that lawyer had to fire him as a client as well.

As you wrap up any conversations with a difficult customer a few other things to keep in mind are to never agree that an employee did something wrong or override that employee who may be in the area watching how you handle the situation. If you decide that you want to override something said by an employee that could not be done make sure you are overly clear that the employee had done everything by the book and that there was no way for them to offer this resolution as it is outside of our policies or company guidelines and you are in fact the one not following the policy to make them happy. This will help save face for you and the employee who was generally just following the rules and policies that you have set in place for these situations. After they leave I would also say that regardless of the situation you must bring back any involved parties to your office to discuss the matter to get their side of the story. I would ask them what happened and why they think the customer was so upset. Depending on the answer I would ask what they feel they could do next time to make sure the same situation did not happen again. If you determine they could have done something or said something differently that could have diffused and resolved the situation on their own, then coach them on it there and make sure they know your focus is for both the employees and the customers to have a great time. Anything that we can do to make that easier on everyone involved is what we want to do. If the complaint had no merit, then thank them for their time and ask them to shrug it off and go have a great rest of their day.

I would urge you to look at these difficult customers a little differently than you do now and try to follow the steps outlined above to help diffuse and come to resolution with these customers a lot more quickly and easily with fewer gray hairs on your head as a result. Remember to never take any of the complaints and yelling personally, and don't allow your people to take them personally either. For quick reference the steps are listed again below.

- Get informed before meeting the customer
- Greet with a smile, offer a handshake, and exchange names
- Ask them to explain what the problem is
- Take notes as they speak, details matter
- Listen with the intent to understand and not the intent to respond
- Thank them for bringing the complaint to your attention and assure them you will act on the matter
- Never offer discounts or compensation unless directly asked by the customer to do so
- Never say that your employee did something wrong in front of any customer or other employees
- If you override policy make sure that you clarify that your employee who may have said no was absolutely right and that you are the one violating policy

- Thank them as they leave and then follow up on the problem to make sure it doesn't happen again as needed

Chapter Seven
Peel Back the Onion
(Effective Problem Solving)

There are always problems that arise in a retail environment whether small or large or any size in between, and you (as the leader) are ultimately responsible for coming up with a solution. Yes, you should instill some forms of problem solving and solution empowerment in your associates, but even when you do this you need to teach those employees how to peel back the onion and find the root cause, so they don't just implement a Band-Aid fix.

Most people like to look at problems and come up with the fastest, easiest solution to fix the problem at hand and just move on. That seems like the logical way to go right? Wrong! While this will get you out of a fire and moving, the problem is very likely to come back up again over and over, depending on the size and severity of the problem and how many people are involved in the process where the problem arose in the first place. Human nature provides the opportunity for choice and choice brings the opportunity for an infinite variety of actions and therefore results to each decision made. This is the problem with quick fixes or Band- Aid solutions. You cannot spend time fighting fires every day or you will find that you are inviting the mindset of you being the "firefighter," and the only one able to make decisions. The quick firefighter solution does not fix the root cause of the problem, and that's what you truly want to focus on—even if it takes a bit longer to be decided.

The way to best look at solutions to problems as they arise is to pause and sit back to really think about what went wrong and why, and then "peel back the onion" to get to the root cause.

Almost always the root cause comes back to one individual person, process, or product that caused the failure and problem in the first place. When you take the time to think about the true causes and trace them back you can now fix the problem at the root, so it doesn't happen again and is a sustainable solution for the future and does not have to waste your time and energy to reevaluate later and time.

Let's look at a few examples and see this in action. First, we'll discuss a situation common to all customer service environments of customer complaints on the service they received whether in person, phone, or even online. The customer has a bad experience and now wants to speak to the manager (you) to tell you all about how horrible the experience was, how much money they spend in a year, and how they are never going to shop with you again (fairly common trend in these complaints to follow this exact flow of statement). You should ask questions and take notes during the complaint to fall back on later as you investigate what happened from your employees' point of view. You as the manager now must address the employee to fix the complaint and are presented with the choice of a quick, temporary Band-Aid fix or peeling back the onion.

A Band-Aid fix would be calling the employee back to your office to tell them they had a customer complaint and then write them up for poor service or just send them back out to their work area and tell them not to do it again without even asking them what happened or why they feel the complaint happened in the first place. Does this fix the problem for this employee? Maybe yes and maybe no, but probably the latter in most cases. The worst part is that the more employees you have and the higher the turnover in staff is on a yearly basis, my bet is that with this strategy you will have to deal with this problem over and over and will never truly fix the problem.

A peel-back-the-onion approach would look a lot more like calling the employee back to discuss the problem and asking them for their version of events first. Then compare those answers to the notes you took from the customer. As you are asking what happened, if they had obvious room for better service or were just plain rude, that is part of the problem. As you dig deeper ask them if they understand what the customers complaint was about. That might open another part of the problem. If they can't see the customer's vision of what service should look like, as you dig even deeper ask the associate what they feel could have been done better. You may find even more parts of the problem. Let's assume the employee told you that they were frustrated with the customer because they had too many questions for them to answer and they were going to be late for lunch. So, they cut them off and said they had to get going. The associate had an attendance discipline record for not taking lunches on time, so they thought they were doing the right thing. As you start to discuss further the associate also brings up that they are always understaffed for the afternoon rush where shifts do not overlap, and it is difficult to spend enough time with one customer while they know others are waiting for their turns as well. The problem could be seen as the associate cutting short and leaving. The problem could be seen as them having continued attendance problems. The problem could also be seen as an understaffed time when complaints are continually come in, or as a combination of all of the above. By peeling back the onion you see an awful lot more opportunities than were originally thought of and can now address each portion of the problem individually for a more sustainable solution.

Let's take a look at another example. Customers are constantly complaining that they were not informed of all the details and options for their orders and, had they known the specifics, they would not have made the purchase in the first place. I've had this in the past and was 100% positive my sales associate had explained to them the process as we train them very well before we allow them to go on the floor to sell to our customers. The Band-Aid fix is to dismiss the complaint as a complaining customer or to just sidebar with the employee to tell them they had a complaint and to make sure they better explain it in the future.

A peel-back-the-onion approach would look more like calling the associate back to your office to discuss the complaint and ask them what they felt went wrong and could have been done better. As you do this you may ask the employee to sell you the service or item as they would a customer to see if they do truly explain in properly or if they really are explaining it wrong. I had this with an appliance sales associate who was telling customers incorrect information on delivery and install procedures. Because this associate was a top seller we just assumed that the customers must not have paid attention or understood as explained. As I asked her to sell me the product from start to finish she made a lot of false statements and did explain the install incorrectly as the customers had stated. When I explained to her the true process and what it should be she told me that she was informed of this process by the old delivery agent and had been telling people it this way for months! The root cause of the problem was the employee was using bad secondhand information and not the training we had given her. She wasn't intentionally doing it wrong. I was then able to fix that incorrect knowledge and make sure it was sold correctly to all future customers.

Let's look at another example. You are down in sales compared to last year in a few specific categories that are not following the trends of other items in their areas. Category #1 is weed killers which are down versus last year and you must come up with a solution as to why. The main drivers of this category are a low-grade item at $19.99 that you determine is actually up in sales over last year. The next item is the same size but is sold at a higher price at $29.99 and is down significantly to sales from last year, enough to drive the overall category down. As you inspect the problem you need to look at all the available information and ask questions to determine what is truly causing the underperformance. In this real-life example in a store I was running I was looking over numbers while walking with the supervisor of the area asking them what they thought. The individual said customers had just switched to the cheaper item. So, they decided to bulk that item out in large quantities to try and help it sell even more. Had I not asked any further and accepted that answer they would have gone on selling the cheaper item and hoping to make up the shortfall on dollars by just selling enough more units of the cheaper item. But by asking more questions and peeling back the onion I was able to determine a few other things that were the real cause of the problem. When I asked why they decided to bulk out the cheaper item versus the more expensive item they told me that customers were price conscious and that it is easier to sell the $19.99 item versus the $29.99 item. I then asked them to sell me some weed killer as if they were assisting a customer in the aisles. When they did so they recommended the cheaper item to start with and then said we also have a few other choices that are a bit more money but this one will work just fine for killing your weeds. When I asked them to explain to me the difference of why the $29.99 item was a higher price they were not able to do so, and when I explained the difference to them they agreed it was actually a much better value than the "cheaper" item. There were multiple parts of this problem that were found by peeling back the onion and looking for the root cause. First, the employees were not trained well enough on the product to sell the differences on a $19.99 item that did kill weeds but only concentrated out to make 5 gallons of killer versus a $29.99 item that was concentrated to make 10 gallons and also had a pre-emergent in it that would keep the weeds from coming back for up to four months! In that scenario the $19.99 killer was actually a more expensive item at $3.99 a gallon versus $2.99 a gallon for the better quality "more expensive" weed killer. The second was an assumption that the employees had made that customers would not want to buy the item based off of price and were what we call "selling with their own wallets" versus leading with the best item for the customers problem regardless of price. The third problem is that they were chasing sales units versus trying to increase average tickets. It is much easier to make up sales by selling an extra $10 on each item versus trying to sell enough cheaper items to make up the difference. i.e., to make up an extra $5,000 in sales you would have to sell an extra 250 bottles at $19.99 versus only having to sell an extra 166 bottles at $29.99. If you sold the same 250 bottles extra of the $29.99 item, you would have made almost $7,500 more in retail sales versus the $5,000 on the lower-priced item. The solution then came to change out the extra bulk stacks of weed killers to the better product and to retrain the associates to lead with the best when selling and use the benefits of that item to sell it and show the customers why it is truly a better option. We were able to pick up the $5,000 missed in sales over the next three weeks and actually raised sales over the following month once we trained the associates properly on how to qualify and recommend the best product. Again, the problem wasn't lack of sales, or poor sales conditions. It was untrained associates with poor perceptions on what to sell to our customers.

When faced with a problem that needs a solution deeper than a basic fix make sure you "peel back the onion" and follow these steps.

1. Identify the problem
2. Research facts
3. Discuss with those involved in process
4. Look for the actual Root Cause
5. Address the Root Cause not the end result for sustained results

Chapter Eight
Delegate and Follow Up Process

This chapter will focus on delegation and follow up and how to effectively use them to get things done how and when you need them done consistently. There is a pretty straight forward process that you can use to make this happen and that is delegate, give time, follow up, then recognize and redirect or reprimand. We'll dive a bit deeper into each area below...

Delegate. Whenever there is something you need done that you are not going to do yourself you need to delegate (give direction and assign a task or tasks) to someone else to get it done for you. When delegating tasks to your team there are a few things to keep in mind. Is this something so important that you need to do it yourself? If so, then do it yourself and do not delegate it. Sometimes you do have to get yourself in the trenches and make things happen. When they are super high level, you might find it best to do it yourself and save the worry of whether it is going to get done and get done right the first time. If you determine that it is something that you can delegate (probably 95% or more of all tasks can and should be delegated) then you need to delegate it properly. This might sound odd that you could delegate something wrong, but trust me. There is a science of how to delegate. First, you need to make sure you are selecting the right person to delegate this task to so that it can be done right the first time. For example, you would not delegate leading a sales presentation a high-level client to your brand-new employee when you have tenured, high-performing employees at your disposal, the same as you wouldn't delegate sweeping the bathrooms to your high-level sales employee. Make sure the task fits the employee's skill sets and abilities prior to choosing them for the task at hand. Next, you need to make sure that you are clear and concise in your direction so that when you walk away you can be sure they understand what you want, how you want it, when follow-up will occur, and when you want it completed. This will save a lot of wasted time on their part trying to fill in the blanks on their own instead of having to come back to you to get more information on what you truly wanted in the first place. This will also set you up for a higher rate of success when you move onto the follow-up stages of the process. If you cannot explain the task within a few short minutes with clear enough direction, then that direction probably needs to change to fit the audience. You want this direction clear enough that if written down and delivered by someone other than you that even a fifth-grader could read and understand the direction and be able to get rolling and complete the project properly.

The next step in this process is to allow the employee or employees the time to effectively get the job done. For example, if you gave them a three-week deadline to get the job done and you are sure you gave them clear enough direction, you may wait a week or week and a half to do a check-in follow-up with them to see how they are progressing. This way they know you have the trust and faith in them to complete the task and you are not hovering over them micromanaging but also gives you enough time to redirect if they are not on pace or the right path to where you wanted them to be. The same applies even on a one-day project where you give them the direction at 8 a.m. and give them a deadline of 5 p.m. to be done. You might not follow back up with them at all until 5 p.m. if it was an easy task or you might want to pop in and do the follow-up meeting around noon to see how they are progressing. You can either initiate the follow-up piece yourself or you can provide direction when delegating the task for them to follow up with you at a certain point in the process. Either way you need to make sure that is spelled out during the delegation step, so it is not a surprise to either party involved when it happens. You need to show faith in your employees and trust them to get it done right, but always must make sure the follow-up piece happens. If you never follow up they will know that deadlines don't truly matter to you when given, they will know that they can get away with cutting corners as you are not going to check anyway, and ultimately you will end up hurting your team results because of a lack of you being engaged in the follow-up process.

Now that you have given what you believed to be crystal clear concrete direction and given them time to get things done on their own and you have done your follow-up meeting, how you proceed from here goes one of two ways. Assuming everything went smooth and everything was to your liking at the follow-up meeting you should provide recognition and thank them for their progress. Tell them to keep up the great work and then let them proceed. You should feel fairly confident in them completing the task on time and can already begin planning the next task for that employee or employees to do when they complete this one. When they turn in the assignment or you go follow up on their sales results from the task you delegated to them you always want to provide feedback. In this case we said it was to satisfaction, so as the leader you need to again provide recognition and thank them for the job well done, shake some hands or give some high fives and then move on to directing into the next project where you would start this process over again from the delegation stage.

On the flip side, what if when you did your follow-up meeting or when they turn in the assignment and it is not up to your standards and what you had pictured in your mind when you delegated the task? First things first, barring just complete lack of ability from the employee at hand, you need to take the ownership of the failure on your hands and assume you either truly did not give out clear enough direction if they weren't able to achieve what you wanted or you didn't do effective follow up to correct the issue before it was too late. Always look to take the blame and make this known to your team that maybe you weren't as clear in your directions as you thought you had been. Apologize that they have to start over or redo it but explain that what was delivered is not what was needed. This can only happen so many times as your team doesn't want to hear you accept responsibility for problems over and over as they will begin to lose faith in your ability to provide the proper direction from the start and will get tired of having to do things a second or third time. So, if you come to the point where it was not done correctly you need to ask what went wrong and whether your direction was unclear, and you didn't paint a clear enough picture or if it was a lack of effort on their part to do it as described. Assuming it was unclear direction you start the process over with new delegation of the assignment with clearer direction, and then give time to proceed and follow up again. You might find it prudent to do your first follow up a lot sooner into the redo of the project or task this time to make sure everyone is now on the same page, so the result will come out right at the end. Assuming it was not your direction and they were clear on what was expected, and they just didn't put forth the efforts needed to achieve the goal then that's where you would move to the reprimand portion of the process. This is never fun but is just as important as the recognition piece as if they feel they can get away with substandard results without recourse then they will continue to more often than not deliver substandard results. You need to sit down with the employee or employees and make sure they understand that you took blame for the potential direction miscommunication the first time and then sat down and redirected them with new understanding of the task at hand and they agreed that they understood and were able to get back to the project. It was not that they were unclear on direction. At this point you must assume it was not that they didn't know but that they didn't care. While this is not always the case and you wouldn't normally want to say it that bluntly to them that you are assuming they didn't care about the results, you do want to make it clear that you do not accept these results as satisfactory and that they will be held accountable for their inability to deliver as needed. You should then move them on just as the last employee or employees who did a great job by redirecting them into a new different task where you can give them a chance to start over and redeem themselves. I can almost all but assure you this time they will put forward better efforts as they were just held accountable for their performance and they do not want to have that happen two times in a row. If they do allow it to happen a second time in a row, then you truly need to help that employee evaluate if this is the right job for them. They are not living up to the standards you require from this position and they might be better suited for another position or, if determined, maybe better suited to work at another company and it's best to cut ties.

Hopefully you can use this in your day-to-day managerial decisions as you decide what tasks to delegate and to whom, goals, and assignments to going forward. Remember to choose the right person for the job first, then make sure you have crystal clear direction to that employee with timelines, expectations, etc. Then make sure to give them the time and space to accomplish the tasks delegated to them, then make sure that you either initiate the follow up meeting or give them time to come to you for the follow up, and lastly make sure you recognize for a job well done or redirect and reprimand for failure to produce as needed. Own your role in the communication process, own your role with providing clear direction, own your role in follow up, and own your role in recognition or reprimand.

Chapter Nine
Surround Yourself with the
Right People

n this chapter, we will discuss the importance of surrounding yourself with the right people and how that can impact your business in a positive manner. When you think of the number one asset or liability of most any organization it is the employees and the payroll they consume and the results that they deliver. Ultimately you want to have a happy mix where you are at your payroll budget and achieving consistent results from your team at the same time. If you are not at your budget and or are missing sales metrics, then your employees become a liability or an expense versus being an asset or an investment in your business. The difference is an employee who cares and is doing their best is an investment in your business because they are providing a return on your investment of time, training, payroll, etc. An employee who does not provide a return on your investment then becomes an expense and whenever possible expenses need to be trimmed.

When many managers sit back and describe what they truly want in their team many times they are not even sure what they need and that's the first setup for failure by not having a clear plan of what personality and abilities you need to be successful in each position in your environment. I always hear, "Well, if I only had a whole team of people just like me or if I could clone my top sales employee we would be killing it!". The problem with that thought is that you would then have no diversity and no matter how good you think you are or even your best employee is if your entire team acted and thought like that employee things would fall through the cracks and success would not come as easily as you would think. What you truly need is a diverse group of individuals that as a whole combine to have all the qualities, personalities, and abilities to be successful.

Think about the different positions in your environment. I'm assuming you have sales positions where people are responsible to drive sales as their main job function. I'm assuming you have customer service positions that are there to answer questions or resolve complaints. I'm assuming you have operational areas such as back office for payroll and accounting. I'm assuming you have freight-handling employees who are responsible to get the heavy lifting done outside of work hours and get the product to the right areas. I'm assuming you have leadership positions responsible to manage and lead certain areas or shifts of your business, and I'm assuming you have cashiers who are there to check out the customers when the transactions are all complete. Think about these positions again. If your top sales employee was placed as a freight-handling or back-office employee, would you get the same results or would this person struggle for human interactions and the desire to close a sale? If you placed someone who isn't detail oriented as a cashier and they were incorrectly ringing up merchandise, that would be better fit as a freight-handling employee. If you had a bubbly personality in the back office handling payroll that should truly be in the customer service area you would be seeing a lot more success and job satisfaction from these employees as well by placing them in the right positions.

It is OK not to be the best at everything in your environment and it is actually healthy to have people outshine in specific areas of personality traits, job function capabilities, etc. As long as you understand where you are strong and where you are weak you can look to surround yourself with those who will complement you and essentially balance you out to your employees. I can tell you personally as a leader I am a numbers-driven guy and I can dig through a pile of reporting, look at sales trends and results, identify up and coming trends and go after sales with ease. What I do lack at times though is the people skills portion where I spend enough time on personal conversations and keeping up with what's going on in the employees' lives. I know for my team to be successful I need to place my second-level leaders (assistant managers) with people skills as a high-rated competency if I want to balance out my numbers-focused attitude with my employees. If I had an entire team of leaders who were just as focused on the numbers versus how their people were feeling and doing, we would see results, but we would also see employees lose dedication and lower morale by leaving their feelings out of the equation. I can also tell you that as the leader most of the time when you are dealing with the employees concerns and complaints you have to be the ear they can bend and the shoulder they can cry on when needed. You cannot go out and be the hammer to your employees or, again, you would lose credibility. For this I make sure at least one of my second-level leaders has the ability to hold employees accountable as a highly rated competency so that when hard things need to be done or rolled out that we have someone comfortable with doing so. I can also say that while I feel I can get into each and every area of my business on a daily basis I can get caught up in the weeds of a problem of the day or week that I am working on solving and I need another one of my second-level leaders to be focused on ensuring we are in line with our payroll budget, our markdown budget, our expenditures and controllable purchases budget, etc., while I am off handling other tasks. This approach ensures that whatever shortfalls I have, or my other leaders have that as a whole leadership team I can always have someone to pull from to be the personality or ability that I need at that time and none of the other areas fall behind.

What I would ask you to do at this point is to grab pen and paper and list the traits you think you would want from each position in your environment by position and by leadership role including yourself as well. When you list out the traits be specific and then rank them as the most important trait down to the least important trait of this position from 1-5 or so (don't get too excessive for hourly employees as they should have a pretty narrow path of skills by position to achieve success, managerial positions will have more as they need extra skills to be successful leading a larger group). Now that you have this list and have rewritten it ranked from top to bottom I would ask you to start from the top and then rank yourself, your second-level leaders (assistant managers), your first-level leaders (department or shift supervisors), and then your top sales or metric driven positions first. You can get to the lower level positions later, the most important ones to focus on first are the leadership and metric driven positions. Now that you have taken this list and you can see where you have ranked your abilities based off what you know is needed to be successful as well as your first and second-level leaders you want to look for trends and areas that have gaps needing to be filled. If you for example rated yourself low in motivation or soft side/people skills then you want to make sure that one of your second-level leaders directly underneath you have that as one of their top-rated skills, if that's not the case then you need to coach it into one of them or when replacing that position as it opens up next time knowing that that is the trait you are seeking in that leader above all others. The same process would then go for your second-level leaders to their first-level leaders, considering whether they balance each other out to where the hourly employees are going to be able to have a full set of skills displayed to them at any given time by the leadership team.

Again, I urge you to look at skill sets needed to drive success and make sure that you seek diversification in those skill sets as you hire and place going forward. You need to fit the skillsets of that person to the position and not try to shove someone into a position they are truly not built for. Surrounding yourself with the right people will lead to better morale, higher employee satisfaction, lower turnover, and a more consistent customer experience as a result.

Examples:

Self (Store Manager)

Important Traits Ranking of Ability

1. Metric Driven (2)

2. Customer Service Oriented (3)

3. Detail Oriented (4)

4. Desire to Win! (1)

5. People Skills (9)

6. Motivation (7)

7. Training and Development (6)

8. Ability to Delegate (5)

9. Accountability (10)

10. Operational competency (8)

Based off this you see that your second-level leaders need to have some highly-rated competencies in Accountability, People Skills, Operational Competence, and Motivation. They can overlap in some areas, but those must be rated highly to balance you out as the leader.

Assistant Store Manager (second-level leader) #1

Important Traits Ranking of Ability

1. Metric Driven (7)

2. Customer Service Oriented (3)

3. Detail Oriented (8)

4. Desire to Win! (5)

5. People Skills (1)

6. Motivation (2)

7. Training and Development (6)

8. Ability to Delegate (9)

9. Accountability (10)

10. Operational competency (4)

Assistant Store Manager (second-level leader) **#2**

Important Traits Ranking of Ability

1. Metric Driven (4)
2. Customer Service Oriented (7)
3. Detail Oriented (8)
4. Desire to Win! (3)
5. People Skills (10)
6. Motivation (9)
7. Training and Development (6)
8. Ability to Delegate (5)
9. Accountability (2)
10. Operational competency (1)

As you can see based off this that leader #1 does help balance you on your lower-rated areas surrounding people skills, motivation, and operational competency so you can count on this person to help keep the employees engaged and happy and act as your cheerleader so to say. You can also see leader #2 is more the "hammer" and focused more on the black-and-white things such as Operational competency and Accountability than the people. This person gives you some added structure and brings a bit of fear to the team to stay on their toes and again helps balance out leader #1 as well. If you do these exercises and see too many overlaps with key areas of competency rated low and no one with them rated highly you need to course correct asap and get someone to take over that trait as the main driver until you can hire someone into that position with it as a skillset going forward.

Chapter Ten
Leaving a legacy

The greatest achievement you can ever hope to have as a leader in any organization is to have people that you have hired, trained, mentored, and helped promote look back and say the reason they are where they are now was directly influenced by you at some point in their career. This is known as leaving a legacy of other leaders behind that will help them succeed as well as the organization to have a solid pipeline of trained and ready leaders for their own future success. I like to look back at the many leaders that I have helped at different points in their leadership development and know that many if not all of them will sit in an interview someday and list my name off as the reason they decided to move up into a leadership role, to say that I sparked an interest in learning more and applying themselves to be the best they could be, and to say that they hope to someday be able to pay it forward and have someone say the same things about them in an interview down the line.

I can tell you the name of the person who did this for me was the 3rd store manager at a company I started out pushing shopping carts at part time while earning money to go to college. His name was Rob and he was a prior military man and was a real hard ass and he expected a lot out of everyone that worked for him. At the point in my career I was in it really wasn't a career but more a part time job that was slightly above minimum wage and I had absolutely no intentions of staying at long term. I had grand plans to do something big and earn a lot of money with the degree I was pursuing and while I put forth a lot of effort into my work I wasn't actively trying to learn more or move up at all. Rob stopped me one day and called me into his office where he asked me what I was going to do with my life. I told him that I was going to college and that I hadn't decided on a final plan yet but that I wanted to be able to afford a solid living for me and my then fiancé as we started a family. Rob then asked me why I wasn't thinking about the store I was working at as a career option and why I wasn't already a supervisor and working to develop a career. I paused for a second when he asked me this question as I honestly had never considered making it a career as it was retail and who makes retail a career I thought. I responded the best I could with "honestly I'm not sure, I had never thought of this really being a career". Rob then told me that he saw a lot of potential in me and had seen me working hard and already being a leader amongst my peers without the official job title and that he would like to see me apply for the supervisor position and then take it from there. I told him that I would think about it but again my focus was about how I could earn a solid salary for my family and I wasn't sure if retail leadership was the path to doing that. Rob kind of laughed when I said that and asked me how much I thought a decent salary was. I replied with $50,000 was what I was hoping to earn after I got my degree, at that point he laughed again and told me even as an assistant manager I could earn that easily and then some with bonus checks, stock grants, and the potential to move up as high as I would like to go without the need for a college degree. He went on to show me his own paycheck at that time which was on track for more than double what I was hoping to achieve after 4 years plus in college and a whole lot of tuition debt to go along with it. I went home thinking about the conversation and discussed it with my fiancé who told me why not go for it now and I could always continue working on my degree at the same time in case it didn't work out or I didn't like it. After that I decided that it made sense, so I went back to work and got that supervisor job fairly quickly after.

I was soon supervising 6 people in a department that was doing $5 million dollars a year and all of the 6 people I was supervising were older than me and many had been there longer as well. I had a lot to learn but I had a strong work ethic and I was smart, so I wasn't really worried about the struggles as I knew I would be able to overcome them with time and practice. I learned a lot from my assistant manager who was responsible to train me on how to look at the business, how to drive sales and understand profit and loss statements, gross margin, markdowns, clearance inventory reduction plans, shrink plans, among about a thousand other things but honestly I don't even recall that managers name at the time I am writing this as they never made an impression on me other than some functional knowledge as I was starting out. Rob on the other hand would come by and would walk me through my areas and challenge me on a daily basis to do better, to sell more, to get more out of my people. I at one point was walked down an aisle that was pretty out of stock and beat up pretty bad and Rob made it clear this was not acceptable and told me to fix it. I spent all night in that aisle and made it look absolutely perfect working an extra 4 hours of overtime to make it happen and I was damn proud of how it looked when I left. The next day I walked right up to Rob and asked him if he had seen the aisle after I fixed it up and he said he had and that it looked great. I was proud for all of about 2 seconds until he asked how I got it to look that good so fast. Beaming with pride I told him that I had spent an extra 4 hours by myself the night prior packing down and cleaning up and wanted to make sure it was perfect before I left. Rob quickly told me that that's where I went wrong and that I had done it all wrong and wasted my time cleaning it up that way as I had not taught my employees any lessons other than if they let it get messed up that I would come behind them and clean it up for them. I was deflated, tired, and just about ready to sneak out of the room to feel sorry for myself when he stopped me and made it clear why he wasn't happy. He told me that this was a learning opportunity that if I was working harder than my employees and if at any time during the day my hands were dirtier than theirs that I wasn't leading them right and managing the department, but I was letting it and them run me. He explained that had I walked one of them through the aisle as he had done with me that when they cleaned it up it would have stuck with them that I would not accept this going forward and if they wanted to avoid having to work extra to clean up what should have been right in the first place that they should never let it get that way again. He explained that I could have done some of it with them to set the tone and example but that I should never go do it all on my own without giving my team ownership. I got it at that point that he was testing me and that even though I was not happy with how he did it he truly did leave an impression and taught me a good leadership lesson that day.

As time went on I was promoted from that first department to a much larger one doing $10 million dollars a year with 15 employees. This was a big accomplishment for me at a very young age and I was confident in my ability to do it with success after all the hard times I had had learning the ropes in the smaller department and all the challenges Rob had given me to prepare me for this new and much larger task. What I didn't know at that time though was I had a lot more learning to do and a lot of harder work ahead of me as I progressed upwards in the store. While I was responsible for just my department and its results Rob would stop me in all areas of the store and ask me questions about what was going on with their sales, what was going on with out of stocks in their aisles, what was going on with their people and he expected me to know it even though it was not my area and I had technically no responsibilities in those areas or reasons to know the answers for that matter of fact. I did not always have the answers but if I did not I would write down whatever I was asked, and I would get an answer for him as quickly as I could. What I learned later was that he was not just being a hard ass and was not expecting more out of me than others as a punishment (as some others who he was not as hard on saw it) but he was doing it to prepare me to run bigger and better departments and to prepare me for being an assistant manager down the road. I eventually ran up to 3 areas at once and was overseeing up to $20 million worth of sales departments at a time! I was also made a key carrier that had opening and closing store job responsibilities and was told that whenever I was in the store I was to carry a manager's phone extension and answer it as if I were the manager on duty at the time. I was thrust into making decisions well above my pay grade and dealing with upset customers, upset employees, and handling the accountability process up to the point of termination as needed. Rob at this point was himself promoted up to be a district manager and was leaving the store to go affect a larger group of individuals than he had access to in the store and with what he had done for me I knew he would do well in that role. I was shortly after that asked to interview for an open assistant store manager position and when I did I knew I was ready for anything after what Rob had taught me.

When I sat in the office with the district manager doing my interview as to why I wanted to be an assistant store manager my answer was simple. I told my story of how when I was just a low-level employee pushing shopping carts I was stopped by my store manager and told that he saw potential in me even when I didn't myself. I told him that as a result I was trained and given the opportunity to become an assistant manager and further myself and better be able to provide for my family as a result of what

Rob had done for me as my store manager. I told him that I wanted to be able to pay it back to future employees as Rob had done for me and that I wanted to leave a legacy behind me to where someone someday would be sitting in an office saying that I had done the same for them in their careers. I did get that promotion and a few years later was promoted to store manager and used the same message to the district manager interviewing me at that point. I was just one of about 15 salaried managers in our district who had been promoted under Rob and we all had similar stories of how hard he was on us and how it had shaped us for what we had become as leaders in our company and how we knew we wouldn't be nearly as good as we were had we not had him in our career pointing us in the right direction. I assure you Rob will have a legacy that outlives him as it is passed from leader to leader through this company and the names of who made the difference will change to hopefully mine as well as the names of other who he has influenced.

You may or may not have this type of story in your history of someone who has influenced your career or life whether it be a manager, a coach, a teacher, a family member, etc. I urge you to take a look at yourself through and understand that if you are not teaching and training your employees and seeking to pull out the best from your top potential employees then you are not leaving a legacy and are just another replaceable manager filling a position versus a leader who is truly influencing their employees and making them want to be better and perform at a higher level. I assure you that I do stop to think about this in my stores that I have been a leader in and who would say that I was the reason they are currently a leader, that would say that I had spent more time with them than others ever have, that I was making a difference in their careers and therefore their lives. If I ever catch myself having a hard time answering this question I know that I have work to do and I can redirect my attentions to a few top employees and get myself back on path to staying a true servant leader who is there to better my employees over myself. I can happily say that I have helped promote many employees from part time to full time, from employee to supervisor, from supervisor to assistant manager, and from assistant manager to store manager! I have had many of them call or email after they have moved on from my store to thank me for what I had done for them and that is a great feeling of satisfaction knowing that they are in a better place and that I had played a part in them seeing more in themselves than they had just as was done for me. Whether your name lives on in infamy or as a legacy of leadership is truly up to you and the choices you make as a leader.

Chapter Eleven
Customer Engagement and Creating Customers for Life

(The Lifetime Value of a Customer)

A s a leader one of your main goals outside of creating a great environment for your employees to want to work in is creating a great environment where your customers want to shop in. A common misconception with a lot of leaders is that they are focused on just the sale in front of them at that time that day and not focused on the lifetime value of the customer as repeat business. When coaching your employees on customer service you want to set this message clearly before they ever interact with their first customer. A great customer experience and that customer will return to your location time and time again when they need the products you sell and would bypass other more convenient options such as e-retail or other local brick and mortar retailers. A poor customer experience and they will not give you the chance to earn back their business generally until they have a worse experience somewhere else.

I would like to throw out a real-life example of this happening to me in purchasing a vehicle. My wife had a very specific car that she wanted and so we went to that dealer and after a fairly decent exchange over pricing and terms we made the purchase and were very happy with the car and the dealership. Obviously when we needed our next vehicle we didn't hesitate to go straight to this same dealer for the next vehicle and didn't even shop around since we knew we had such a good experience there the previous time and they were in our minds honest and straightforward so why would we? Well after a much harder sales negotiation than the previous experience we finally agreed on a monthly payment and down payment and signed papers and were on our way. On the way home though I did not have that same warm and fuzzy feeling as the last time and it had me go over the contract with a fine-tooth comb when we got home because something just didn't seem right. Upon investigating it I found a $1,500 "government donation fee" had been added to the contract after our initial round of negotiations which I was never made aware of. I immediately called the dealer to ask what this was and was told that the monthly payment I had agreed to was actually higher than what it would have been, so they added the donation fee to round it up to that payment amount. I was livid and asked him to explain to me why he wouldn't have just come back out and said, "great news, we can actually get you a lower payment and wrap this up right now!". He assured me this was common practice and wasn't sure why I was so upset. I asked for his manager who basically blew me off and I ended up having to email the regional vice president of the company to set up a meeting to go over my concern where he finally just told the dealer to write me a check to make me go away. I was happy to get my money back but was so upset that over the next 5 years I steered more people away from that dealer and to other dealers and at a minimum cost them $100,000 in total revenue that I would have happily referred and/or spent with them.

The mistake they made was focusing on the one-time sale in front of them and not the lifetime value of me as a customer. That extra $1,500 was worth it to them to lose over $100,000 in sales and that's obviously a horrible business decision and one that I'm sure they made with many other customers. Over the course of that next 5 years the dealership was sold to two different owners and eventually closed before being reopened in a different location after building such a poor customer service reputation. I am not sure how they are doing in that new location but can tell you as a consumer that I would still not buy from them even after changing hands so many times as I have found a new dealer that has treated me fairly and there is no reason to go back to them.

You need to instill in your employees that the customer may be in shopping for ideas and pricing today that could turn into a lifetime customer or could be in ready to close a 5 or 6 figure sale and both are just as valuable as each other. In my current business we have an average ticket of about $60 and an average lifetime value of $125,000. I teach my employees from day one at orientation that each interaction they have with a customer regardless of that purchase that day will either earn us or lose us $125,000 and if they treat every customer with that in mind that they will go far and do well knowing that without the customer we don't have a business and the customers are ultimately who end up paying their salaries.

One of the best things I would suggest that you do to coach and train your new employees on the value of the customer is to do role plays and observations. Role plays are when you have them sell you something for practice and you get to have an interaction with them on how they would be selling and speaking to your customers. This is a great time to recognize them for things they do great such as greeting, qualifying, recommending, closing, as well as coach them on a few points they could emphasize or do better in to close the next sale easier or to have a better shot at adding to the average ticket and upgrading the customer for their project today. An observation is when you then watch from a distance how they do with real life customers in a selling situation. Things to look for are who initiates the conversation (should always be your employee and not the customer), whether they follow the greet, qualify, recommend, close selling process, and whether or not they can actually form a relationship with the customer and close the sale in a short period of time. This feedback is a lot better than the role plays because you can see what really did or didn't work and coach them for the next opportunity and watch it again to see if they pay attention and improve. I love to ask my employees when they walk away from a customer to tell me about them. If they can tell me what the customer was working on, what the next project they had in mind was, etc. then I high five them and congratulate them on earning a customer for life. If they cannot answer those questions or just tell me they were looking for a single product I get the opportunity to coach them on true customer engagement and finding out what they are working on as a whole, and not just a single transaction. I then remind them of the lifetime value of a customer to our store and ask them if they feel they earned the repeat business or not. This is not an everyday coaching statement but really can push the message home a bit harder than them thinking small scale about the single transaction today and focusing on the lifetime value of that customer and the people they influence.

Today we rely on social media more and more and people when in an unfamiliar area or looking for an unfamiliar product will generally seek feedback of where to get that one of a few ways; Google, asking a friend, or a service such as Yelp. What would you find if you pulled up your location on yelp to read reviews? Would you see many 5-star reviews commenting on employees by name and suggesting everyone come to you for whatever it is you sell, or would you see the 1- or 2-star reviews telling people to stay far, far away? Most people unless they feel strongly one way or the other are not going to take the time to write a review and those who are feeling strongly enough the write one are generally geared more towards the negative side and are not only going to blast you on yelp, but twitter, Facebook,

Instagram, or whatever new social media service is out at the time. One bad service experience could not only cost you the lifetime value of that single customer anymore but it they influence 30-40-50 or more others in seconds at the push of a button on their phone or computer you could be losing potentially hundreds of thousands or millions even if hit hard enough.

You as a leader MUST ensure that your people are living up to the values you expect for customer service with every customer, every time. I like to tell my associates that when they start any engagement with a customer that they are only going to see them as an employee and recognize them as the uniform but by the end of that interaction I want them to know them by name and thank them for their help. A customer for life is much more likely to be created by someone going home to rave to their friends and family about how great "David" was at the store they shopped at today and if you ever need anything with this product then you should go see him versus them just saying they liked the store location. On the flip side of that statement the customers are never going to go home to rant about never going to see "David" at that store, but they will say never go to that store period. You have to get an awful lot more customers for life than losing as an employee for me and even one or two lost can be detrimental to your location's survival.

In closing on this topic treat every customer like gold and set the example early and often for your employees on what you expect from them in regard to customer service and provide coaching and development to perform higher and higher. Whenever possible recognize those who do a great job and commend them on creating a customer for life and not just for closing the big sale of the day. As a leader you hold the keys as to which employees you allow to engage with your customers and you must understand that outside of your associate retention and safety the next most important thing is how your customers perceive this employee and if they are making the decision easy on them to want to return again and again. If it's a positive perception, then awesome you are doing a great job! If it's a negative perception you need to take the accountability to the next level with this employee and fix the situation before they are allowed to lose you a single additional customer.

Chapter Twelve
Be an Active Listener

The role of a leader changes every day depending on the situation in front of you and the people that you are working with, the problem you are trying to solve, etc. One thing that never changes is the role of the leader to be an active listener. While you may think that just sitting down with an associate and letting them vent or having a performance conversation with them and not saying anything while they are speaking is "listening" to them but unfortunately it is not that simple. An active listener needs to "listen" with the intent to truly hear what the other person is both saying and feeling and not respond in a way that makes the person feel you had an agenda and whatever they said was unimportant. Think back to your last conversations with your current leader, did they look you in the eye, did they keep typing on their computer or looking at their cell phone, did that cross their arms, did they ask questions to clarify meaning, did they really listen to you and make you feel like your conversation mattered? You will build a lot of trust and loyalty by being an active listener or you will lose a lot of respect and faith from your employees if you don't follow these tips outlined below.

1. **Paraphrase.**

Once the other person has finished expressing their thought or opinion, paraphrase what he or she said to make sure you understand and to show that you are paying attention. A few ways to paraphrase include "What I heard you saying is..." "It sounds like..." and "If I understand you right...." Try not to be over the top with this or they will feel like you are condescending but be genuine with your response.

2. Always ask questions.

Whenever I have a serious conversation I always try to ask questions to encourage the other person to elaborate on his or her thoughts and feelings. Avoid jumping to conclusions or making judgements about what the other person means. Instead, ask questions to clarify his or her meaning, such as, "When you say_____, do you mean_____"? You can also use questions in general conversations to show active listening such as "How long have you been into (Hobby)? or "When did you first become aware of _____"? a few simple questions show you care and are listening.

3. Show empathy and emotion.

If the other person voices negative feelings, seek to validate these feelings rather than questioning or defending against them. For example, if the employee expresses frustration, try to consider why he or she feels that way, regardless of whether you think that feeling is justified or whether you would feel that way yourself were you in his or her position. You might find it helpful to respond with some things such as, "I can tell that you're feeling frustrated," or "I can understand how that would cause you to feel frustrated." Again, you don't have to agree with why they feel the way they feel and sometimes you will feel strongly against it. Never disagree or tell them what they are feeling is wrong, you are just acknowledging at this step and can hopefully get them on your side later in the conversation. Your role as the leader though it to make sure they feel that you at least understood why they felt the way they felt.

4. Be aware of your body language.

Body language can play a big role in if the employee believes you are listening to them and care about the conversation. You can show that you are engaged and interested by facing the other person, maintaining eye contact, nodding, taking quick notes, and maintaining an open and relaxed body posture. At all costs avoid all potential distractions such as checking your phone, reading or responding to emails, or even looking at your watch. Whenever possible if it is a serious conversation invite them into your office and close the door and place your phone on your pocket or better yet tell them you are going to put it on silent upside down on your desk to show them that you are the only priority you have at that moment. Be aware of your facial expressions and do not display any expressions that might communicate disapproval or unacceptance. Things as small as your feet and full body not facing the person can show disinterest as your feet are pointing you away from and out of this conversation. Stop yourself and face them full on and give them your full attention. I have found this one hard to do and you may need some practice to stop letting body language emotions show through.

5. Take turns. Don't overpower the conversation.

After the other person has had a chance to speak and you have participated in an active listening conversation it will be your turn to respond. Make sure before you are responding that you have given a fair amount of time for them to be finished speaking so they don't feel you were cutting them off or just waiting for your turn to speak and respond. It is sometimes best at this point to ask them if they mind if you give them your thoughts so far and make sure that you are both on the same page. I can tell you many times after I gave my recap of what my thoughts were that they had calmed down and were satisfied at that point that they had truly been heard. I use this step to gain respect and if needed turn the conversation back over to them as many times as needed.

6. Do not reply with advice.

(at least not right away)

When a problem is presented to you whether by an employee or a difficult customer the last thing they generally need or want is for you to respond with a solution or advice as soon as they finish speaking. When you do this, they may feel that you were not actually listening to them and instead formulating a response while they were still talking. Most people want to be heard first and foremost and know that they were heard. When it comes to for the actual problem-solving it is likely to be more effective after both participants understand one another's perspective and feel heard. This is a great opportunity to paraphrase and then ask them "What would you see as a fair resolution"? or "What would you do if you could make the decision yourself"? this shows you trust and empower your employees and that you are open to any suggestions from the other participant whether employee or customer. You may agree with the solution if you think it is fair or you may suggest something similar by again asking a question such as "What do you think about _____ as a fair solution"? that way you are not "telling" them the solution but receiving their buy in on agreeing to it.

7. Pausing and silence is OK.

Many people find silence and pausing uncomfortable and try to avoid them at all costs. I would tell you in an active listening situation that a pause and silence can be the best thing to show that you are truly listening to them and taking time to process what was being said. If you respond too quickly as I stated above, they will feel like you were just waiting for your chance to respond and not actively listening. When you pause and let the silence play a role in the conversation you will find that it helps to calm tense situations, shows engagement and consideration to their feelings, and shows that you are not trying to rush the conversation and get yourself out of the conversation. Pausing can also help you gather your thoughts and make sure that what you say when you do reply is what you actually mean and will be received properly by the other person based off their current state of mind.

While not every one of these steps will come into play in each and every conversation the more you practice and are aware of your own personal reactions and conversation traits the better prepared you will be when a truly difficult conversation comes up. Even the best leaders out there have active listening as one of their worst traits that they wish they could improve in as well as their employees wishing they would improve in. I challenge you to have a conversation with your significant other, a friend, a neighbor, or a peer and see how many of these traits they display now that you are aware of them and how many you catch yourself with room to improve. Practice is the only way to improve on listening and trust me you will need practice and it will be well worth it.

Chapter Thirteen
Retail is Detail

(Compare Yourself to Perfection)

This chapter may be a short one as it is a simple topic but a very important one for all brick and mortar locations. You have to remind yourself every day that your customers have a lot of options on where to buy the products that you sell, and you have to give them a reason to shop with you and more importantly your location if you are part of a chain etc.

If you walk into a grocery store on a general day you will see products faced to the front of the aisles, cleanly swept floors, prices on every product, clean fresh produce, a cereal aisle with every box pulled forward to perfection, etc. You come to expect this when you shop there and if you walked in and saw it in disarray and steaks on top of chicken in the meat section and mold on the tomatoes would you shop there again? Of course not, you would know that there is a problem there and they no longer care about the products that they sell or the customers they are selling to. Whatever it is that you sell in your location whether it is in person or online your people need to know the details of the product and how to sell it and how to keep it clean and presentable to the next customer.

I like to use the grocery store example when I am walking my stores and looking at the aisles. I can recall many coaching sessions where I called over the employee or manager on duty at the time and asked them to tell me what they see in the area I am unhappy with. Many times, I would get an excuse and a response of how it's not that bad and I'm just being a perfectionist. I would generally then throw at them the question about what if this area was a fruit and vegetable section at the grocery store? Would you buy fruit that was out of place and on the floor? Would you be happy to purchase a damaged and taped back shut box of cereal? Would you shop here again if this was your first-time experience shopping here today as a customer? If they cannot answer yes (which they generally don't) then I explain to them how important it is to have the details right every day for every customer. I will say that I understand things happen and areas can get out of line with standards and expectations but if that happens then they have to have a sense of urgency to get that area back up to standard quickly before too many customers have to shop in an area not ready for business or in "Grand opening ready" condition. Most people get this but a reminder and you having consistent and clear direction when you see things out of line will dictate how well they keep the areas when you are not around.

I want to call out a couple things in retail where "retail is detail" are very important. I have come to call them the 3 P's of retail so when asking an employee or manager what are the "3 P's" they have to recall them and explain what they mean. The "3 P's" are Product, Placement, and Pricing.

1. Product

Product is about making sure your product is in the most optimal condition possible. For example, if I'm selling peaches am I going to showcase the bruised ones or am I going to cull them out and have only the best available for my customers. Maybe I still sell the bruised ones, but I would want to separate those away from the perfect ones as not to detract from the value of them. It's hard to see a perfect fruit as still perfect when next to bruised or damaged fruit as you expect them to have come from the same place and what happened to the other one could happen to the perfect one as well. This is never good for instilling confidence in purchasing decisions with your customers. Have the best products available at all times and make sure they are in a clean neat orderly display. Same idea would be a pile of peaches on the floor versus a pile of peaches in a nice display. Which are you more likely to buy from? Seasonality would also come into play here. If it is summer and you are trying to showcase and drive sales on rain boots, then you are not focused on the right product. Focus on the product that has the most seasonally relevant ability to sell and you will see much higher sales results.

2. Placement

Product placement comes across in a few different meanings. One is the literal placement of the item for sale and the other is the placement of suggested selling items around the core product. If it is fall season and you are clothing store more focused on showcasing your summer line of swimsuits that you need to sell out of at the front versus having high margin seasonally relevant items such as coats and scarves and gloves at the front, then you are not following the rules for product placement. You want to always showcase the most seasonally relevant products and higher sellers with better margins when possible at the front of the store, at the front of the aisle, at the front of the department, or on the home page depending on your business. As or even more important than placing that seasonally relevant items in the most visible location is to get accessory selling items as close to them as possible to make whole package purchasing easier on your customers. The easier that you make the purchasing experience the more you are likely to sell to each customer. If you had the products scattered around where they have to hunt down products to buy together especially when in what we would call "off shelf" or out of the normal home location for that product then we are making it too hard on the customer. If you have a display of toilets then have the toilet seat there with it, the supply line, and the wax ring. If I have to go hunt down those other items, the chances that I miss buying one or all of them skyrocket and the sales loss is a result of the person who merchandised the items with poor product placement.

3. Pricing

You may or may not have any control over the actual pricing of your products that are in most cases unless you are running your own location set by the corporate office you do have the ability to showcase pricing and values on your own. I would say at a bare minimum you should have an expectation that every item on display in your location will be expected to have a price on it, so a customer never has to ask or question the price of an item. If most customers don't know the price they are more inclined to just leave it there and not ever ask so this is crucial! The next step in pricing is to showcase values! I would like to throw out for example a pricing on a sale item. If you saw an item that was $99 and is now $79 with a sign that reads "Save $20 through Tuesday!!" that is a whole lot more exciting to me as a customer and would influence me to buy it now versus a sign that just says $79. Same could go for an item that is not on sale but maybe you just know is a great value. I have many times taken items that I knew were below market pricing and done what we call "Dare to

Compare" signs on them where we would call out our price of say the same $79 as described above versus Walmart at $99! "Save $20 versus our competition!" There are also time savings you could shout out such as "installs in half the time" or bonuses such as "FREE 3rd year warranty when purchased by 10/12!" Look for ways to make the ok seem exciting! You cannot do this with every item so try to go big on anything you off shelf or showcase and use it to drive your sales higher than others with the same product and placement but not as exciting "Pricing".

While it may sound cliché and you will for sure get some eye rolls if you say it out loud it is true that "Retail is Detail". Small things can and do matter to your customers and the more you can make your offering stand out versus your competitors the better foot up you have over them even if you have the same products at the same pricing. If you have the best product in the right place with the right pricing (showcasing the value) and friendly knowledgeable employees available to assist why would your customers even consider shopping somewhere else?

Another thing that comes along with retail is detail is comparing yourself to perfection. When you look to benchmark yourself against a goal there are a lot of ways that you can look at it and set that benchmark. Maybe you base it versus your sales plan, or versus last year's comp sales, maybe it is versus your closest competitor, or maybe it is versus another location of your same business if in a chain and you have access to that information. What I would tell you is that they are all valid ways to look at your performance but there are no better ways to compare your performance than comparing it versus perfection.

How in the world do you compare performance versus perfection? What in the world does perfection even look like and how can I define that in a book? Well, perfection is just that; perfection. Perfection is when you can take all the variables and know that you didn't leave a stone unturned in your search for "perfection". It is easy to claim a win when you did 10% more business than last year, but is it really a win when you know you were under your hours budget and had many items out of stock? Was it really a win when you know while walking the floor that you had employees not engaging with customers and actively seeking to drive a positive sales experience 100% of the time? Was it really a win when you had one specific area or product or customer drive your performance to the 10% comp and you had others in flat or negative comp performance? While I don't want to take away a win when it is absolutely a win I do want you to think of the opportunity that was left on the table had you executed to perfection.

The "detail" or "perfection" in this example can be applied to anything from people, displays, cross merchandising, training, sales, performance reviews, etc. You must always look to remove any "disclaimers" or reasons to make your performance sound better than they are even if good enough and look to take "good enough" to perfection.

I used to have a leader when I was an assistant manager that would have me report out my previous weeks business every single Monday, and every single Monday regardless of how good my performance was whenever I shouted out a big win he would always come back at me with a smirk on his face and ask "and you are satisfied with that?". It got me every single time and I would almost always say no, we could have done more but this is still a solid number. He would then ask me if I just said we could have done more, then how could I call it a good number? This went on for months and it took a while for me to realize he wasn't trying to tell me that I was doing a bad job or not living up to standards but he was trying to get me to realize that while I was exceeding goals I wasn't executing to the level of perfection possible and there was always something more I could have pushed for and gone after had I not accepted beating a goal as going far enough. I then took this example to my assistant managers when I became a store manager and when they would proudly tell me they hit 100% of a goal such as their new credit card goal for the week I would ask them if they were satisfied with that. I would get a variety of reactions from shock to the question and a resounding yes to a quizzical look as if a trick question and a no response that they could have absolutely done more. I would always come back at them and ask if they were sure that we didn't give up when we hit 100% then I was happy with the result, but if we did let off the gas then we hadn't executed with the goal to achieve perfection and deliver as many as physically possible and we were just trying to hit the minimum acceptable goal of 100% to plan. As a leader you have to recognize the win but still challenge to execute to the fullest and be as close to perfection as possible.

Chapter Fourteen
Control What you can Control

n retail as with any business there are things that you can control and things that are completely out of your control no matter what you do or how hard you try. What you need to focus on understanding here is to put your efforts and energy into controlling what you can control and not putting your time and energy into what you cannot. The challenge is determining what you can control and what you cannot and how to do so in a quick manner.

When you think about external and internal factors in your business as a leader if you were to list them all off it could take hours if you really dug down to the deepest details and they will change day to day and especially season to season. Within your control could be things such as labor costs, the number of hours you are open in a day, the people that you hire, the items that you sell, the places you showcase the items for sale in your business, the promotions that you run, your return policy, etc.... Things that you cannot control could be things such as the weather, competition opening up in your area, road closures, major political events such as rising minimum wages or who is elected as president, tax rates, legal restrictions on items for sale and shipping regulations, age restrictions on items for sale and or even the ability to sell certain items, etc.. Then there are things that are in a sort of grey area that "could" be controlled by you or "could not" be controlled depending on how you look at them. I would throw things into this category such as your sales in a day, the attrition and retention rates of your employees, the call out rates that you have, customer foot traffic on days when no external forces have drivers on them such as weather or major events, repeat customer business, customer referrals, overriding policies, etc. What I would like to focus on for now is ones that fall into grey areas as these are the ones where you can turn them into ones that you can control versus things outside of your control if you put the right mindset and efforts into doing so.

When I stated a few of the things that could be considered grey area I used a few examples and we will hit on a few of them here and see how you could turn them into a controllable event versus an excuse on an uncontrollable outcome. There are a ton of other examples that could be used, and I urge you to come up with a few specific to your business after reading this section and think about how a mindset change could turn them into a controllable situation going forward.

1. Sales in an average day.

You might look at this one as an uncontrollable event because you cannot control what customers come into your location and how much they spend when they are there right? Well I would challenge that thought and ask you to think about the things that you control that would lead to higher sales in that day. Can you control whether or not you engage with every customer that walks into the store that day? Can you ask them open ended questions with the intention of figuring out what they truly came in looking to buy and more importantly what problem they wanted to solve? Can you do suggested (consultative) selling with them and add to the overall average ticket for the day by upgrades and add on items to increase your overall sales? I can say that be doing the above properly you absolutely have control of what your end of day sales are each and every day and if you miss your run rate then you at least know that you did everything in your power to get it where it needed to be. Far too often I would hear from associates that there weren't enough people to hit their goals for the day or week and that people were in just buying small cheaper items. When I challenged them to increase on these areas and spelled out that just a few dollars added to each average customer adds up tremendously eyes were opened, and they started to pursue sales with a stronger passion especially on slow days because I had changed their mindset.

Example of one of those conversations: My store had missed sales plan for the week by $40,000 which is a HUGE number when you look at it at first glance. I then asked my leaders to tell me why we missed plan and got all kind of excuses that ultimately just shows they were in the "victim" mentality of bad things happening to them that they didn't deserve and not that they could have controlled the outcome had they wanted to. I then asked them to break out the reporting and some calculators and we were going to do some math. I asked them to get me three numbers; the overall sales miss, the number of customers that had been in the store that week, and the number of hours that we had used for labor that week. We already had the $40,000 sales miss so when they came up with 15,000 customer transactions and that we had used 3,400 hours we were able to then do some math and determine that we had actually missed sales plan by $2.67 a customer or $11.77 per hour of associates working. When I threw those numbers at them and asked them if they truly believed we could not have controlled adding just $3 a customer or asked each sales associate to do an extra $12 in upgrades or add on items per hour they worked that we would have made up and crushed that $40,000 they were shocked. I then got a lot of wide eyed leaders who said when they looked at it that way that it was our fault and in our control for that miss and that they would definitely be able to go challenge their associates to go add $3 a customer this week to make sure we made up for last week's miss and wouldn't you know we did closer to $5 increase per customer that next week and made up all of the miss in sales and then some. It is your responsibility as the leader to make unsurmountable goals such as this "out of our control" sales miss easier to achieve and change the mindset of your team away from the victim mentality and move them over to the winner mentality.

2. Associate attrition and retention rates.

While many people look at labor as the number one expense on your P&L (Profit and Loss statement) they don't always look beyond the black and white numbers on paper and look at them as actual individuals and either value added or value detractors and expenses to your business. When I first started out as a leader I never really thought or cared about associate attrition and retention rates, hell I didn't even know what they were when I first started out as a leader. Attrition is the number or percentage of employees that you lose or turn over in a year and retention is the number or percentage of employees that you retain. If you have a team of 24 people on average and you lose and replace just 1 a month that is equal to a 50% attrition rate as half of your staff would change out every year, if you lose 24 in a year it's as good as saying a 100% turnover is to be expected for the coming year as well. I will cover this in detail a bit later but know that this is bad and will absolutely cost you money and customers the higher it is. Now, back to is this something you can control or not. If you treat your employees fairly, pay them fairly per the market, and give them a voice in your business you are doing things that drive retention and help the number of employees looking to leave to be at a minimum. If you don't spend the time to get to know them a bit better than just as an employee and more as a person (see finding what motivates later in the book), if you don't hold underperformers accountable, if you don't try to work with their home life schedules when possible then you are not controlling your retention and are in effect controlling adding to a higher attrition number because you are not giving them a reason to stay with you. I like to say that if someone is happy with work and who they work for even if not happy with pay they will stay there and not even look elsewhere until they are no longer happy with who they work for (you as the leader). You can and do control this metric as well as how often they call out or leave early, what efforts they put into work when there, etc. by engaging with them and being a true leader versus being a boss and treating them like numbers on a piece of paper. If you feel this is still out of your control or blame it on wages, etc. then you need to take a longer look in the mirror and determine if you truly understand the value of your employees and your role as the leader in their retention.

3. Repeat customer business and referrals.

When a customer shops with you and your employees as a reflection of your business you get the chance to either earn a customer for life or lose a customer for life or make literally no impact on them at all. When you say that repeat business is out of your control you could be right if you are again looking at it from the victim mentality, but if you look at it from a winner's mentality then you would find the ways that you could say lead to positives here. Can you control the customer service you give when the customer is in your location today? Absolutely! You will find that interaction and engagement from your employee will absolutely determine whether or not this customer wants to come back and definitely whether or not they would recommend you to a friend or family member should the conversation come up.

Can you control when they come back? Maybe... If you have a solid marketing program or loyalty program for them to sign up for and you actively drive sign ups when in your building, then yes you can control when by being at the front of their mind when you shoot out messages or emails or mailers and if they recall back to a positive experience when in last they will be much more likely to come back and shop with you again. Treat every day like you are trying to win their business for life or at a minimum for trying to earn their business for the next purchase each time they are in shopping with you. You unfortunately will not be the one interacting with each and every customer so your employees need to be the ones driving this with each and every customer and as a leader to make this a win and turn it into a controllable event you have to recognize and reward top talent and great examples of service when you see it, you need to be on the floor soliciting feedback from customers every so often and thanking them for their business, you need to have a recognition program in place for peers to recognize peers for doing a great job, and just as important you need to hold those accountable who are not part of the winning game plan on your team and would be turning this into a negative in your customers minds. Even the best employees who see another employee putting up poor efforts and service levels who is not held accountable and corrected or removed will eventually drop their level of performance to the lower "accepted" levels of performance.

Why try harder when you can get away with less? Hopefully you never have that thought as a leader, but you need to know your employees will have this thought should you allow it to come up.

As a leader you control a lot of things and while there are things that you ultimately cannot control you have to take your best efforts to turn uncontrollable into things that you can control or at least control the things that lead to the outcomes of the things you don't think you can control as demonstrated with the above 3 examples.

You control who you hire and when, you control how you treat your employees and your customers, you control the condition of your environment, you control the friendliness of your employees, you control the sales abilities of your employees, you control the influence you have over others, you control how engaged you are in your business, you control how engaged your other leaders are in their business, you can control more than you can possibly imagine as a leader if you put forth the efforts to take control. If you ever find yourself thinking there are no ways to impact or control the outcome or situation then stop, breathe, and peel back the onion to all aspects that influence the outcome by writing them all down and checking one by one and I'm sure you can find at least a portion of the process that you can impact and start there.

Another thing that you have full control over is your decision-making abilities and what trust you place in others to decide when it comes to your business. As a leader you will at times have to make decisions that you cannot leave up to your employees to make. While you want to empower your people to be problem solvers and come up with their own solutions things come up that you just have to make the final call on whether it be a personnel problem, a large pricing problem, a seasonal change out, etc. When it is time to decide and you cannot allow your people to come up with the solution and decision on their own you need to act with urgency and make the decision without over analyzing and fear and uncertainty. If you are afraid to decide, then you are effectively making the decision to do nothing which can be just as bad or worse than a bad decision so why not take a swing and see what happens?

One of the worst traits a leader can have in the eyes of their people is being wishy washy or indecisive. Your average employee will not have the desire or trust in themselves to make decisions and they will come looking to you to make the decision for them. If you make up your mind but then change it or think about it for too long you show a weakness in decision making to these employees and they will lose faith in your ability to make decisions properly in the future. You must have a consistent ability to stick to a decision and show strength in doing so without fear of failure. Most decisions are fairly easy to make and don't take that much entrepreneurial courage, but others will test you a bit more and that's ok as long as you take control and make a decision. Worst thing that happens is that you were wrong, and you have to pivot and make a new decision. As long as you admit this to your team and have given ample time for the decision to play out they will not hold it against you.

As a closing note on this topic controlling what you can control does not mean micromanaging, it means being aware of all possible outcomes and doing everything in your power to make sure that the things that lead to "wins" are in place and your people know what is expected of them and have the tools to succeed with your support and leadership. You don't have to be involved in every decision or situation, but you need to make sure your team understands what your expectations are should that situation arise, so they can execute with the intent to succeed and do it right.

Chapter Fifteen
A Person is not a Process

To get anything accomplished in a consistent manner you need to instill processes and procedures for your employees to follow with straightforward guidelines. A process is the act of writing down a structured set of steps, quality controls, and expectations of how and when to get these tasks done. The problem many new and old managers alike fall into though is that they are not good at coming up with these processes and instead rely on a person to get things accomplished. While that can be ok for some small things you really must implement a process that can be executed by anyone who may need to with similar results. When you rely on a person and not a process you will get inconsistent results and that will cause extra follow up and headaches on your part which is unacceptable and completely avoidable.

Let's look at a few examples of things where a person or a process are being utilized and see how they differ and why a process is always better in the long run.

A common task among almost any business is opening and closing the store or office for the day. A process in place for doing so would look like a list of items that any employee new or old could follow along with and check tasks off as they go to come out with the same results on a daily basis. These employees would need minimal training and once they have learned the process you have little to no follow up needed on this area as they know the expectations, they know the order to do them in, and they can easily explain the process to a new person as needed to get them up and running. I'm sure you will have someone that currently is doing this exact task for you right now and they are probably doing a pretty good job, so you feel comfortable with them continuing to do so for the foreseeable future. What happens however if this person has a family emergency and needs to leave for a week or longer? If you don't have a process in place with backup people trained to do the same task with similar efficiency you would have at that point not had a process and been relying on a person instead. When you rely on a person you will always be at the mercy of not only that person's performance but also and more importantly at times just their presence! At this point when you get the call at 9pm that the person responsible to open the store/office/whatever at 5am is not going to be there and you have to turn to panic mode. Hopefully you at least have a person you can move shifts to make it work but what happens when they have never done the opening shift and don't know the process for how to clear the alarm system, how much money to put in the registers and in what denominations, how to unlock which doors at the right times, how to complete any safety or compliance checklists required, etc.. You now must retrain this person on the fly and hope they get it close to right with minimal impact on your business.

On the other side what about if it were the person responsible to close down your business? This person is generally the one who would make sure that the aisles are swept, that the empty boxes are taken off the shelf and replaced with fresh product, they walk each closing employee through their area and make sure that it is ready for the customers who will be in first thing at open and it is up to standards. If this employee were not there and you did not have a process in place for the replacement employee to follow to make sure each and every area of importance is up to par what would your comfort level be then? Would you expect minimal impact to your business with the change over the following week or would you be worried about it affecting cleanliness, in stock levels on shelf, decreased associate productivity, decreased customer satisfaction, and decreased sales overall? Had you have had a process in place for specifics on what is expected from this closing manager and how they are to do it your discomfort level would be minimal as a result of the initial time investment of training the process to the right individuals. When something goes wrong you cannot be upset at the person who was not trained to do the task at hand as you were truly the one responsible as you never put a process in place and trained backup employees incase this were to happen. Think about this even on a more micro level with your current leadership team and if you notice differing levels of performance, appearance, sales, productivity etc. by manager when they work different shifts I'm assuming you don't have a consistent process in place for your team to be able to deliver the same results. I would also assume that you do not have this process spelled out in writing that you could hand off to the new person to reference as they took over that role. Which would you rather have at this point, a person or a process?

All right, opening and closing a business may be a pretty straightforward task you say, and you don't think that's a very big deal. Well what about your sales process? I'll speak from experience on this one and use a real-life example. One of the most important things to any business is sales obviously and understanding how to keep these sales coming in and how to increase them any chance you can. At this specific company we had something we call "leads" for services provided in home for our customers whether by our company or a third party we would submit the "lead" to for follow up, contact, and hopefully closing the sale. A fairly simple process it would seem to just interact with customers on a daily basis and then collect their information to submit a lead and sit back and collect the sales. The problem was any lead generation business is only as good as the process you have in place to collect quality leads for customers hot to buy. We had one employee responsible to ensure we were hitting our goals weekly as far as leads by specific programs with different goals on each one. This employee was supposed to go around the store training other employees how to offer the services and how to get the customers to give us their info for a free no obligation estimate and then follow up with them on a weekly basis to ensure that they were in fact signing people up for these leads. Whenever this person was in the store things were great and we were hitting our weekly lead goals consistently and as a result were meeting or exceeding our sales goals for these programs regularly. Life was good and there was little to no follow up needed on my part as a result, so I focused on other more pressing opportunities across the store.

Well, wouldn't you know when this person took a vacation we would see a drop off significantly in leads and the excuse from my leader over that area was always that her lead generator was out on vacation and we would make it up the following week. When I explained to that leader that she was putting all her eggs in one basket by running this business with a person and not a process she understood and assured me she would get a process in place to make sure we had the other employees more engaged with this process, so we wouldn't see any drop offs again in the future. As time went by this employee responsible for these leads started having health problems and was missing work more than she was at work and as a result we were falling off the face of the earth as far as our lead performance was concerned and as a result of that our sales began to decline as well. This was completely avoidable if we would have truly implemented a training and follow up process for our employees to be trained, tested, and held accountable to a weekly or monthly lead goal after we were confident in their knowledge of programs offered. The person was doing great and as a result we got complacent and didn't worry about the underlying process and cost ourselves tens of thousands of dollars in sales as we struggled to put a band aid fix in place as we implemented a new process that wasn't relying on an individual person to execute and deliver the results. The process going forward was changed to have the lead generator responsible for the same lead metrics as before, but we also put a training goal on top of that to where they had to train a minimum of 10 employees a week on a program and challenge them to generate a lead of their own. The "process" then continued to ensure that at least half of all leads generated were from different individuals each week, so we could count on a variety of employees contributing and not just that one "person". This led us to sustained success with very consistent results and were able to transition between multiple future lead generators over the following years without any hiccups in transition. We peeled back the onion to find a root cause and then formulated a plan that we could delegate and follow up on and control what we could control with a process. (See how it all ties together)

Whenever you have a process in place you will see similar results regardless of what individual you place in that role as they will know the ins and outs and have clear and concise expectations. Whenever you have a person as your process you are opening yourself up to failure and unnecessary reliance on this one individual and their performance. I urge you at this time to think about your team at this moment and what would happen if you were to lose your top or business operating critical people in any variety of positions and what would happen tomorrow if you had to move forward without them. Do you have a process in place where you could quickly and easily train someone to take over with minimal business impact or would you struggle and have to reinvent the wheel with each new employee in that position? So, what do you do if you have a person and not a process and how do you fix that and fix it quickly?

The first step I would tell you to take is to go to the individuals who are in these key positions that are lacking a process and meet with them one on one. I would explain to that person that you are very happy with their performance and the contributions they make to the success of your team. This will work to build some extra rapport and confidence with the employee and make the next part go a lot smoother. I would then ask you to tell them that you are so happy with their performance that you want to get some feedback on how they are able to do specific parts of their job duties so efficiently, so you can see if you can cross those tips and tricks over to other areas of the business. This will let them be upfront and open with you on how they get things done without feeling like you are asking them to write the roadmap of how to replace them with someone else with this new knowledge and process. You will be able to then take these tips and tricks and write out a detailed structured process of how any individual in this position would need to be able to step in and deliver similar results. I would also ask you to partner them with a backup employee to have them train them for taking over on their vacations or sick time, so they don't have to ever worry about coming back to a mess. This again will lead to better results on a consistent basis and you will have at least two people at all times trained and ready to follow the process and deliver the same style results. You can use the written process with this new backup employee and ask them if there is anything missing from the list that they would add to it that they learned from the "expert" who trained them and update it from there. You will then be able to train new employees to do this process at your current and/or future locations with ease.

Chapter Sixteen
4-Step Sales Process

There are a million different ways for a salesperson to approach sales with their customers and a million different ways that customers respond to those tactics. The point of the 4-step sales process is to provide a simple but highly effective base guideline for your sales team to follow so that they can better engage with your customers and help drive sales as a result. This process works great when teaching those new to a sales environment, but even the most experienced salesperson could use a refresh on these topics to stay on top of their game. The four steps are Greet, Qualify, Recommend, and Close and we will look at each one individually in this chapter. Your role as a leader is to teach these steps to your sales team and help coach them on how to improve using the following information. Remember you cannot be mad at someone for not hitting sales goals if you haven't given them the tools to succeed in selling to your customers and not everyone is a talented natural born salesperson and needs to be coached on this as a learned skill.

Step 1. Greet

Whenever you are dealing with customers in any sales environment you should always be the person who initiates the contact and greets the customer. When you walk up to the customer in a non-confrontational manner and greet them with a smile and your name and if comfortable offer a handshake to start off the interaction. The sales process goes a lot smoother when you are the one to initiate the conversation and offer your assistance versus them having to find you and ask for help. When you greet with name it should look something like this. "Hello, my name is John, what brings you in today?" or "Hello, my name is Sally, I see you are looking at our appliance sale, how can I be of assistance?" These are very non-confrontational and are not pushy with a what can I sell you but more open ended and will be more likely to engage in a further conversation. If your employee is not the person to initiate the contact, they can still save the greet step by apologizing for not being readily available and then roll right into a positive opening statement along with their name to again make it more personal. Either way when you offer your name you make it more reasonable for them to give you their name and you can then refer to them by name for the rest of the process whenever possible. Imagine the difference of if you were to introduce them to a peer or a decision maker in a sales process and you say, "this customer is interested in..." versus how it would sound if you were to say, "Mr. Jones here is in the market for a new....". This step cannot be faked and when you greet you must do so with sincerity or the customer will be able to tell and will be turned off if they feel you are greeting them off a scripted process. I like to tell my salespeople to have a few go-to greetings and tailor them to the type of customer they are going to engage so they have a higher chance of creating a bond and engaging in further conversation. If you don't get into an engaging conversation your chances of a great sale are going to be greatly diminished.

There are times when the customer refuses to engage in conversation from the start and is "just looking" today as they like to say. Whenever you get that answer your team needs to be able to overcome the obstacle and stay engaged while not overpowering. The best response to this just looking answer is "That's great, I'm glad you decided to stop by today and take a look at what we have to offer. My name is John and I wanted to make sure you know I am here to assist you whenever you do have any questions." If you have a sale running or a value proposition to throw at them at this time sometimes that can help initiate the conversation from them that will turn into a conversation even though they originally declined it. I have used these many times with my team in an appliance or flooring sales area where I would coach them to then say "I just want to make sure you are aware of the big sale we are running that is ending today (or whenever it is ending) and how it works. If you look at the price tag you can see the original price as well as the sales price so you can take a look on your own as you are looking through the showroom, but what the sign doesn't say is that we offer free delivery, free installation, free haul away, 12 months no interest on our credit card as well as our price match guarantee that we will meet or beat any competitor out there and we can even pull up prices for you online to prove we are the best before you make a decision. Feel free to take a look around and I'll be right here when you have any questions.". You would be surprised at how many people would hear all the great things they were not aware of in that value proposition that would then start asking questions about a part of the sale and how to take advantage of it even though they had just said they don't want help and we had just told them we were going to give them the space to shop as they had requested. If they still don't engage with you then give them space and, in a few minutes, feel free to re-engage and offer assistance again. Whatever you do, don't hover! Give them the space they need but stay visible and straighten a shelf or dust an item off, so they see you giving them the space they wanted but still available to them.

As the leader your role in this is to help them practice. You can role play, you can give them live customer examples, you can have them write out a list of 50 different ways to say hello and initiate the contact but whatever you do you need to make sure they are comfortable and confident when you put them out in front of your customers. If they are super green at sales a fun challenge is to send them out into the store or even to a mall to go hand out flyers and to practice greeting as they hand out the flyers. Don't allow them to come back to discuss how the exercise went until they have handed out all the flyers that you have given them and if available watch from the background to make sure they are actually trying to use the training you gave them and are doing more than handing them out and just saying hello. This exercise is easy and will break the ice before moving on to the next step that is quite a bit more involved.

Step 2. Qualify

When you have gotten past the introductions and you have them willing to engage in conversation you then move on to the qualify step. In the qualify step you need to ask as many questions as needed to truly determine what product or service the customer truly wants for the final outcome of the purchase. Your salesperson should be focused on the customers true wants and needs and not what products they can push onto them as this will be obvious to most customers if you are not acting in their best interest. Imagine walking up to the salesperson at a car dealership and you tell them you are there to buy a decent used car for your daughters first car and they try to talk you into going over to look at a brand-new car that they can get for a similar price. You may or may not be interested in the new car even at a great price, but I am sure you would not be happy that the salesperson shut down what you told them you wanted without even asking any qualifying questions such as budget, mileage, color, transmission, etc.... You would be a lot more open to the conversation of the upsell on the new car if they had engaged in some conversation and asked what your daughter's name was, whether or not she played sports or any extracurricular activities, if she would be carpooling with others, if you had a budget in mind for payment, etc. Your sales team needs to start with get to know them questions and then engage in conversation as they ask the remainder of the questions. Your salesperson cannot just rattle off a list of questions and get to a recommendation, they need to engage in an actual conversation between questions, so it feels like a two-way dialogue and not an interview or interrogation. You need to find out why the customer intends to make this purchase, the "why" can come into play greatly as you look to make your recommendation in the next step by making that recommendation custom tailored to solve the problem or meet the need that the customer has in their mind. You also need to find out timeframes as to their purchasing decision and when they need to make the final decision or receive the product or service, so you can again use that when you make your recommendation in the next step.

Your role as the leader is to make sure your sales team is genuinely interested in the customers purchase and is treating them with respect in their conversation. You need to help them practice qualifying a customer with both sides of role playing in which you pretend to be a customer with them as well as observations of real-life customer interactions. I have found it fun to make a game of this step in training with sales people by having a profile of who I am as a customer typed up and ready to use so I can check mark each item the salesperson asks me about and then see if they use those facts to make the recommendation to me more personalized. If you are able to turn over a paper at the end and show them how they could have used specific facts about you as a person or specific facts as to the who, what, when, where, why of your purchasing decision to make it easier then it makes it easier for most new salespeople to understand and tie these facts to an ability to sell when they see it on paper. You can then ask them what your profile person's name was, why they are in looking to make a purchase, how old the item they are looking at replacing is, whether or not there was a timeline for needing this product, etc. Once you have coached your team to ask questions with what I like to call a "natural curiosity" where the questions flow naturally in conversation then you have achieved success in this step.

Step 3. Recommend

This third step of recommending a service or product is extremely important and the success rate will rely on how well you executed the first two steps of the process. You want your team to be able to recall personal facts and answers that the customer gave them in the inquiry step so that you can make a personal recommendation that the customer feels is in their best interest and not your salespersons best interest. You want the conversation at this point to come across to where you are stating back to the customer reasons why the recommendation you are making is why it is best for them and what they truly want and providing the best value for their money. For an example let's use the used car purchase again and see how involving personal details can make it an easier conversation. I would want it to look something like this "Well Mr. Jones based off what you've told me I'm positive we have a car that will fit your needs and the needs of your daughter. I really feel like the best option for you both would be to look at one of our new base model cars due to the fact that you would have a full 5 year warranty included at no extra cost so you would have the peace of mind while your daughter is out on the road and still be well within your budget of $200 a month if we choose one that has been sitting on the lot for a while that I know my manager would be willing to make a deal on. Plus, we have better financing options and rebates available to get the payments even closer to what they would be on a used car that are only available on the new models through our branded finance department. We can still take a look at some of our used options if you would like but when I think about your concerns such as future trade in value, low mileage, warranty, and safety features I know you would be happier with the new car." This recommendation was not pushy and used reasons that the customer had told you were important to them in making their purchase. You also left the door open to looking at the other option of the used cars but put some reasonable doubt in their mind as to why bother with the used car if it won't meet as many needs as the new car would. Now on the flipside if after you spoke to this customer and based off the inquiry step you determine the used car is the best option for them based off their desire for a cash out the door price or very low monthly budget, the fact that they wanted lower insurance premiums, the fact that they know the daughter is a bit reckless with parking and they don't want to worry about her scratching it up and hurting the value then your salesperson needs to make the recommendation for the best used car for their needs. This would look something more like this "Well Mr. Jones based off what you've told me I'm positive we have a car that will fit your needs and the needs of your daughter. I really feel like the best option for you both would be to look at a used 4 door sedan due to the fact that your daughter will be carpooling her siblings and you will definitely get cheaper insurance rates on a 4 door as well. We do offer an extended warranty option that we can have added on to give you peace of mind while your daughter is out on the road and still be well within your budget. I have a great low mileage trade in that just came onto the lot this week if you would like to follow me right this way." This was again very low pressure and addressed their concerns and the reasons why this customer is looking to make the purchase in the first place. The customer will feel at ease knowing you are addressing their needs and not yours and still gives you the chance to add on the extended warranty to meet the customer's desire for a reliable form of transportation. Whatever you do in this step make sure your team follows their recommendations based off what the customer wants and ties what they recommend to those reasons. It is ok and actually suggested to ask the customers if they agree that these were the right needs you are meeting with the recommendation before moving on as if they agree then you can know you have them on the hook with the right product or service. Make sure to never sell with your own wallet or based on what your salesperson feels is expensive. I assure you there is nothing in this world sold anywhere that is "expensive" just different items for different budgets. I have sold $65,00 bathroom remodels that I would never ever do in my own home, but it was what the customer wanted and met their needs, so we presented the offer and they were happy to make the purchase. If I would have made the recommendation and sold with my own wallet we wouldn't have met their needs and they would have gone with someone else who would sell them what they wanted.

Your role as the leader for this step is to continue along with the role plays and real-life observations to see if your salesperson is using facts to base their recommendation on and if they can effectively tie them together with confidence in the suggestion. Your role is also to help them overcome objections and get back on path if the customer does not like the recommendation for any reason at all. If the recommendation offered is truly the best option for the customer, then you need to reinforce why this is the best option and if they still object then take it off the table and move on to the next solution or offer for this customer. Any sale is good for business as long as the customer is happy and would return and recommend you to their peers especially in this social media friendly world that we live in today where your good or bad service can and will be known by all within seconds of pulling out a cell phone to post a review. You want your team to act as if every interaction is going onto their own personal brand website and that the suggestions they make are truly the right ones for the customer. Don't force a higher price or fancier option on the customer if they don't want it or you will be violating the rules of this process and won't get the opportunity to move on to the 4th step to actually close the sale.

Step 4. Close

This is sometimes the hardest step in the process because it involves you physically asking the customer for their hard-earned money and to commit to making the purchase with you. Why this is hard is a mystery to many, but I've found from experience that people like to sell from their own wallets and would themselves be uncomfortable pulling the trigger on the purchase many times due to a price they feel is "expensive". I want you to make sure that your team understands in this step there are a lot of ways to fail and only a few to be successful. If your team is going to be successful they need to be confident in their conversation which should be easy based off them making the proper recommendation based off the right inquiring questions. The salesperson needs to take that confidence and present the offer to the customer and then "assume the sale". Assuming the sale is basically assuming there is no other option for the customer other than saying yes and making the purchase. Your salesperson should say to the customer something along the lines of "I appreciate you coming in today to shop with me and giving me the opportunity to serve you. The total for what you've got picked out is going to be $xxx and I can get you checked out right here and, on your way, as quickly as possible. How will you be paying for this today?" You didn't ask them to say yes or no, you assumed the sale and you asked for payment! The number one mistake other than selling with your own wallet is to not actually ask for the sale. Imagine the difference in conversation if it went without assuming the sale "I appreciate you coming in today to shop with me and giving me the opportunity to help you with your project. The total for what you've got picked out is going to be $xxx, is this something you would like to move forward with?" Now you have opened the door up to indecision and gave them a chance to say no, or that they want to go home and think about it which you should know has a low conversion rate of returning to actually make that purchase. When you assume the sale, you assume they have already agreed based off your conversations and meeting their needs and you know that this is the right thing for them. They can still say no or let me think about it as they would if you hadn't assumed the sale but when you make the decision easy for them and just ask for payment the customer is more likely to just move forward and make the purchase if it truly does meet their needs. People do not like to make decisions and if you don't agree with that think back to the last time a group of friends had to decide on what to do or where to go eat! The first person to make a suggestion generally wins as everyone else finds it easier to just agree and go along than it is to have to make a decision on something else. Be confident and ask for the sale!

Something that is a great thing to add to this chapter is using "Value Propositions" when closing the sale. A "Value Proposition is when you explain to the customer why going with you on the project regardless of pricing is the best thing for them to do and spells out any other value-added benefits you offer that maybe your competition does not. A great value proposition could be available financing for an installation of the product you are selling especially if you offer any no interest terms along with that financing. Sure, they could use a competitor that may be slightly cheaper but isn't the ability to finance it with you and have no interest for 12 months' worth the value added? What about things such as using licensed, bonded, insured and 50 state background checked installers for that same job? I would sure want to know that the people I am letting into my home are safe to be there and that is definitely a value-added proposition if the competition does not offer the same. Maybe your location has a built in 2-year warranty when the industry standard is just 1 year, doesn't that provide value? I would urge you to come up with what value-added propositions your sales staff could use to close the sale and add extra "value" to use you for the purchase without adding additional costs. Use these "value propositions" to make yourself stand out from the competition and put peace in the mind of your customers.

Your role as the leader here is to make sure that your sales team is fluently comfortable asking for money and able to overlook any price point as an expensive option. You need to help them practice, and practice, and practice again closing the sale as if you do all the great things before this step and you don't actually collect any money then what's the point of it all and you are for sure not going to hit your sales goals without it. Role plays are valuable here and I strongly suggest you throw different objections at them even if they do assume the sale properly and eagerly await your approval. This will happen and the way the handle the objections will determine if they should be in a sales role or not. Can they pull back details and reasons for why this option truly does meet the customer's needs? Can they provide a tangible reason why the customer should buy with you versus a competitor? Can they put a sense of urgency on making the decision today before the customer leaves? Make it simple on your team and your customers, take away decisions and assume the sale.

Chapter Seventeen
Consultative versus Transactional Selling

Whenever you are dealing with customers in any sales environment you are either having a consultative or a transactional sales exchange. The differences between consultative and transactional are immense and can make huge differences in the way your sales results accumulate and the quality of your customer experiences. We'll dive into each one and what you can do to take advantage of both as you coach and train your sales team how to use them to be more successful.

A transactional sales interaction is where the customer requires little to no assistance to make the purchase and can make the purchase on their own many times without a human interaction. These transactional purchases could be something as simple as going to the store to buy a gallon of milk or even going to the mall to buy a pair of shoes. Customers in these scenarios do not expect to receive much if any assistance and have little to no expectations as far as how the purchase is going to go other than wanting to go in and make the purchase and then get on with their days. Your sales team has some pretty basic things they can do to assist in increasing sales using this type of purchase even though they may not ever interact with the customer. First, for the customer to make the purchase, your team needs to make sure that the product is in sufficient stock for your customer demands and on the shelf so that the customer can walk up to the shelf where they know it to be and be able to grab it and go. If the item they came to purchase is not on the shelf and they have to hunt someone down to see if they have it in the back, it turns the purchase sour quickly as this completely blew their expectations of having an easy grab-and-go purchase. Your team needs to make sure you have a solid selection but not to the point to where it gets confusing on choosing between too many items. Your team then needs to make sure that the items on your shelves are in neat and clean condition and have clear prices on them, so the customer can make an easily informed decision on what they want to buy and what the price will be at the register. Last you need to make sure that they can quickly and easily checkout at the register even if that is a self-checkout machine and they still have no human interactions this can still be a great transactional interaction with your business as they were able to get in and out quickly and you met every single expectation of a "transactional" sale.

You may say well if it's just a transaction then how do I as a leader do more than keep it in stock on the shelf? A great example of driving increased sales via the transactional sales process was a study done by a major retailer on an everyday item found in most homes; Tylenol. This company set up hidden cameras and focused them on the painkiller aisle in a grocery store that had as you know a ridiculous amount of choices stretching over 18' of aisle space and then watched and studied customers purchasing habits. They found that while people came in to the aisle with the obvious need to make a purchase they quickly became overwhelmed with the amount of choices of both brand and size and spent over a minute picking up and comparing different options on the aisle and only a very small percentage of the customers actually left the aisle with a bottle to purchase and those who did overwhelmingly picked the smallest cheapest bottle of whatever brand they chose. Most customers went away empty handed after being frustrated with the decision they had to make and even though they obviously needed and wanted to make a purchase it was easier to decide to let someone else deal with the purchase and leave without the item they came for. They then used this info and cut the product selection down to just a few brands with three different bottle sizes and then sat back and watched the customers purchasing habits again. The customers came into the aisle and cut their shopping time in half yet the overwhelming majority that came into the aisle that did make a purchase still purchased the smaller bottles of whatever brand they chose and while there was a significant increase in the percentage that made a purchase there was still a high amount of shoppers that left the aisle without making a purchase that were still unsure what bottle to purchase. Thinking of how they could simplify this transaction even further for the customer they took the selection in their own store to just two bands, a name brand and a house brand and gave both just one large size bottle available for purchase. The same camera setup was put in place and then they sat back and again watched the customers shopping habits to see if this made an impact on the purchasing as they thought it would. The customers now spent only seconds looking at the two bottles and almost everyone that came to make a purchase left the aisle with a bottle and since there was only two brands with the same large size bottle the purchases not only increased significantly in the number of purchasers but also the dollar amounts purchased by having the larger size bottle only available for purchase! This process of simplifying a transactional purchase item to make the decision easier on the customer was a fantastic implementation and took the headaches away from making a decision on brand, size, and price down to an A or B decision that lead to increased customer satisfaction with the purchase experience and increased sales for the store.

As a leader it is your responsibility to think about your environment and areas you can make simple transactional purchases both easier on your customers as well as increase your overall sales. You need to follow the basic principles of having enough of the items, the product on the shelf, the items priced clearly, and an easy checkout experience. You can follow the steps outlined above and put your own spin on it even if you were not willing or able to cut down on sku selection by working on your off-shelf merchandising opportunities. What if you were to have a product of the month up at the registers that has 5 choices in its home location but where you set it off shelf in the secondary location you select just the higher priced item to place in a convenient location and see what it does to its sales. What if you were to pick an item such as a drink to place on a high visibility end cap that had accessory skus that you could place with it like a cooler and make a sign that says "Don't Forget the Ice!", you are now turning a transaction purchase into an increasing average ticket by "selling the whole project" or "completing the purchase".

A consultative sales interaction is where the customer requires some form of assistance to complete the purchase and cannot make the purchase on their own. The range of assistance can vary from very simple such as asking one or two questions like what color paint the customer would like mixed and whether it is for the interior or exterior of the home to very complex such as choosing what layout, design, box construction, door style, stain finish, knobs, faucets, countertops, backsplash, and installation services on a full kitchen remodel purchase. You can see how both required a form of consultation and a recommendation from the employee on what the customer should be purchasing. The way you and your sales teams take advantage of the consultative steps before you begin selling to the customer will determine your close rate and your average tickets as well.

Let's take a look at the first one that we said was on the simple side of an easy purchase such as paint for a bedroom of the customer's home. This sounds like it is a quick-and-easy transaction and funny why we would care about what happens when a customer wants to buy some paint because paint is paint right? Wrong! When you go to your local home improvement store, I challenge you to choose a color and ask how many different skus of paint bases that color can actually be mixed in. I can tell you there are generally at least 9 different bases a paint could be mixed in ranging from $9 a gallon to $52 a gallon and there truly is a right paint within that lineup for each different customer. If your sales team treats this as a transaction versus a consultative process you will lose out on available sales opportunities to increase on average ticket as well as customer experience when they go home to use that paint. The differences between a $9 can of paint and a $52 can of paint are huge in both the quality of paint coverage per coat as well as the ease of application and the smoothness of the paint once it has dried. If you use the $9 can of paint it will require a primer before application which adds an extra step, adds extra dry time, adds extra clean up time of your paint brushes and rollers used to apply that primer as well as a minimum of 2 coats with dry time in between coats as well turning a few hour paint job into an entire day or more project! What kind of customer experience are you delivering when the customer goes home and deals with all these hassles and time added steps to get the job done versus if you had sold them a higher quality paint to start with. The $52 can of paint is a paint and primer in one which saves the customer both the cost of the added can of primer but also the application and dry time of the primer step as well as only requiring one coat for true coverage so only one application step and one clean up step getting the job done a minimum 66% faster than the cheaper paint! What is this customers experience when they are done painting and are on to enjoying time with the family or whatever other project they had to do versus with the cheaper paint where they would have literally been sitting there watching paint dry?

So, you may be thinking that great consultative sales is telling the customer to buy the most expensive product and why it is the best out there and, unfortunately, it is not that simple. To truly have a consultative process you need to first engage the customer and find out what they are looking for in the end result and then base your recommendations based off what they are trying to accomplish. If your customer walks up to the counter to order the paint they wanted and your salesperson doesn't ask any qualifying questions and just starts at the top the customer is going to be turned off and think you are in the process of trying to gouge them for as much money as possible and that you have your best interest at heart versus theirs. When you start off with questions like where will this paint be going? What is the size of the room? What color are the walls currently? Do you have any concerns with the scrub ability of the paint for fingerprints or crayon clean up? I would assume you would like to get the job done with as few coats and steps as possible? Then when you have all of those questions answered you can base your recommendation off of what they have told you in their responses to your inquiring questions. Now when your salesperson says that they would recommend the $52 can of paint because it will go on with just one coat saving you time and steps and will have the best ability to hold up under scrubbing for clean up the customer will know that you have truly sold them something *they* "need" versus what *you* "want" to sell them. They could also say that based off answers that came back to the desire for budget over time that they would recommend the $25 can of paint that will cover adequately with two coats but still save the primer step and then give the customer the option to make that purchase over the $9 can versus going straight to the cheapest option. Also, when they start the actual mixing process while the customer is waiting they can take them over and sell them the proper applicators and prep materials to apply the paint. I will tell you if you make recommendations based off what the customer wants then they will be more willing to spend up over what they had initially intended to spend since they are now making an informed decision based off your consultation. What's the extra $10-20-30 a can of paint worth if done right? Assuming a meager 500 gallons a week that's anywhere from an added $260k-$780k a year in increased sales on the paint average ticket let alone the potential increases of selling the proper applicators and prep materials that could add another $260k or more if used properly.

When looking at this "simple" consultation it gets a lot more involved now that you look at it in this light and you can see how applying this to even larger purchases could make the difference in your customers feeling like you are trying to "sell" them something versus you trying to "help" them make an informed purchase. Your goal as a leader in any consultative sales process is to teach your employees to use open ended questions and to truly pay attention to detail in the qualifying step so they can make customer specific recommendations. Then make sure that you do role plays and get them practice in using the tools you have taught them, so you can provide feedback on whether you feel like they are "selling" to you or "helping" you make an informed purchase. As a leader you then need to give them time to practice this with real live customers and have either yourself or another trained person there to back them up if needed and then provide feedback based off the real-life interactions as they happen. I assure you that your employees will feel more comfortable offering the higher end products as well as your customers feeling better about their purchase and experience when the transaction is complete if you practice and follow this advice.

Take the time to evaluate your business and what you sell that is transactional and what you sell that requires a form of consultation so that you can separate how you attack driving sales with each one of them. Your role as the leader again is to help your employees deliver as much sales as possible and help them feel comfortable about how to do so especially if they are on any form of commission-based sales. Clearly define what you sell transactional that you can make easier, and clearly define what you sell that you have opportunity to consult the customer and upsell so your sales team how to make the most of both.

Chapter Eighteen
Have a PHD Mentality

As a leader you need to ensure a lot of things happen on a day to day basis and that can be difficult at times. An easy way to help things move along in your environment on a consistent basis from both your first-level leaders and your hourly employees is to instill a PHD mentality into as many of them as physically possible. So, what is a PHD mentality you ask? PHD is an acronym that stands for Poor, Hungry, and Determined. Regardless of whether things are going good, bad, or indifferent having a PHD mentality will keep you in the best shape for success specifically with your top-level sales associates and well as first-level leaders who are responsible for delivering results.

P is the first letter of the PHD acronym and stands for Poor. When you are Poor you don't generally have all the daily necessities and are not able to keep up with the Joneses, you are urgent to do whatever it takes to put money in the bank so that you can buy food, pay bills, keep a roof over your family's heads, pay for medical treatment, etc. When you are poor you have to work hard for what you get, and you sure don't take that for granted as you start to achieve success so will work even harder to keep it that way, so you don't go right back to being poor again. Hopefully you have never been down to your last dollar and living paycheck to paycheck but know that can and will happen to a large portion of society and how people react to this shapes who they are as individuals. While some of these "poor" people will accept defeat and accept the fact that they are poor and will stay poor the majority are pissed off that they are in this situation and are going to fight tooth and nail to get themselves out of it. You need yourself and your team to act like they need the results as if they were "poor" and they would not have a paycheck on Friday if they weren't putting forth their best efforts. When people get complacent and accept results for what they are and are not pushing for more they have lost this poor attitude and need to get it back as quickly as possible. It's fine to be ok with winning, but what happens when you have a slow day, a slow week, or a slow month and that winning feeling goes away? Having that "poor" mentality would have kept you and your team pushing to stay ahead and build a buffer in case of down times so you could keep winning alive.

H is the next letter of the PHD acronym and stands for Hungry. A "Hungry" person is literally starving and hurting for more: More food, more success, more money, more career advancement etc. A "hungry" person will be more aggressive than a well-fed person because they have to go out and earn the desire that they seek—and it is not readily available to them without effort. The well-fed person is happy were they are, they are not worried about pushing for more as they have food in the pantry, they have money in the bank, they feel they can move ahead as they see fit and it will require little or no thought or effort on their part. This well-fed person put in the face of adversity will not be able to adapt and react as fast as the hungry person will as they have let that part of their personality lie dormant and were content with things going as things go. The hungry person on the other hand is ready for adversity as they live it every day and their minds are sharpened from doing so and are able to more quickly and easily come up with solutions and resolve to overcome the obstacle in front of them. You want your team to be hungry for MORE! Whatever that more is, is up to you and your team. Do you want them to be hungry for more leads for potential business and not slack off when they have hit their quota, do you want them to be hungry for more sales even though they have already exceeded sales plan, do you want them to be hungry for career advancement to where they are going to work harder than the next guy or girl looking for that same advancement opportunity? Whatever you hunger for go after it and have the mentality that there is always room for more and if you aren't hungry enough to go out there and get it yourself there sure will be some other person who has the hunger and will gladly come eat off your plate if you allow them to do so.

D is the last letter in the PHD acronym and stands for Determined. A "Determined" person will never give up and never accept less than they know they can achieve. A determined person will figure out a way to make something happen and will not give you excuses for why they failed or why it's not possible to achieve the result of the challenge set forth in front of them. You need your people to have the mentality that if they are determined enough to achieve success then they will achieve success and that it is fully within their power to influence the results of their efforts! A person who is not determined will look for all the excuses in the world or will want to greet every challenge with a list of why it won't work or how the timeline is unreasonable. This undetermined person will go out and attempt the task at hand already with the mentality that it's not possible and they are expecting to deliver poor results so will not work as hard to achieve them from the start and are just waiting to say they told you so. A person however that is determined will look at the challenges given to them with optimism and will brainstorm how to best achieve success before they set out on the journey. A determined person will look for ways to answer the reasons others give for why they cannot achieve the goal with reasons they have that may work or different ways to try to make a success more attainable. This determined person will NOT accept defeat and will push up to the last minute for both themselves and their teams even if they are falling behind and the outlook is bleak. When times are good people don't have to be determined to succeed as all ships rise in a high tide and even complacent people will achieve success. When the water falls and its harder to navigate treacherous waters only those with a mentality of being focused and determined to win will find a way through to the finish line.

Having a PHD mentality you will find can be a skill or a talent but can be had by anyone that puts their mind to it and is willing to work harder, faster, and longer than their peers without the motivation to do so. You as the leader have to have all of these mentalities and must always work harder than your peers if you want to stand out from the crowd. I urge you to look upon yourself and reflect to your current self and team at this time and ask yourself who amongst your team is currently acting like they are poor and their jobs depend on their performance, who on your team is acting like they are hungry for success and that they desperately have the desire to win and that they would go unfed if they were not doing so, and who on your team is acting like they are determined to find a way to win and will not accept anything less. Due to human nature you will unfortunately never have a full team of these people but as long as you can keep yourself, your leaders, and your most important results driven position employees engaged with these mentalities I assure you that you will find a way to win more often than not and when tides rise for all you will still be ahead of your competition that is content with being average.

Chapter Nineteen
Hire the Best and Create a Culture
(Associate Retention)

As a leader in any organization especially if retail the number one cost you incur is your payroll and the costs associated with the hiring and firing process. While payroll and employee costs can be considered an expense or an investment one thing that is a fact for sure is you would much rather hire less and fire more. There are some up-front and easy things that should make this pretty apparent to you as a leader but hopefully this chapter will shed light on a few not so obvious reasons to put a lot more up-front energy and investment into your staffing selection and retention process.

As a leader you are ultimately responsible for who you hire and who you allow to stay employed with you after that point. When you look at all aspects of the staffing selection and retention process one of the ones that many leaders struggle with the most is hiring the right people to start with and then getting frustrated when they don't fit the position or company overall for that matter. I have heard way too many leaders in the past talk about just needing a "warm body" to fill an open position and would basically hire the first person that interviewed and could pass a drug test. I would time and time again watch that leader struggle to achieve results and would end up turning over the position again and having to start the process over once again with another "warm body". If you want to succeed as a leader you have to surround yourself with the best talent possible for the position you are needing them in. I would challenge you to stop and think about this before you do your next interview and think what skills this person needs for the exact position I am hiring them for and make a short list that you can check off as you interview. If this person does not meet the needs that you currently have it is in your best interest to pass on them and move on to the next interview. The number one thing you need to do to improve your business and retain better talent is to hire the best! Never ever settle even if it means hours or days of more tedious interviews, get the right person for the job and train them well and it is worth the up-front investment in time to get them onboarded properly.

Once you have that right person selected to be hired I would challenge you to confirm with yourself if you have set them up with the right expectations of you as a leader and make sure they truly do fit. I will generally finish my questions and at the end if I felt good would run down the specifics of the positions that I was hiring for and ask them to tell me which area they felt they fit best in. You would be surprised the amount of people that interview for a sales job that will tell you at the end that they are shy individuals and not really outgoing and that they would honestly fit better in a cashier or labor position. If you run through the position and give them your expectations for customer service, attendance, safety policies, self-directed ability, and what you expect them to do in their "down time" you will then find it much easier for them to come out of the gate running should they pass the final questions as they are officially onboarded. Once you onboard and go over specifics in your orientation you need to again revisit these expectations and their specific roles and routines you want them to follow. Clear and specific expectations at interview and then again at orientation will make your expectations much easier for this individual to follow and try to execute once they hit their actual position and begin to do their job.

The next step in this process to ensure they are off and running properly and you then retain this individual is to have a weekly check in if even for just 10-15 min once a week for the first few weeks and then again for a more detailed sit down at 30 and 60 days to verify that they understand policies and procedures, ask them how they are feeling with their position, coworkers, department or shift leaders, etc.. These check in's give that employee an easy way to address issues without having to have the courage to go chase you down and ask to talk to you which most would be afraid to do so on their own had you not created that culture of openness from the start. Prior to implementing this check-in process myself, I had the worst attrition or loss of associates in the under 60-day category and knew I had to do something to address it. Once I set these hiring, onboarding, and 30- and 60-day check-ins in place, my under- 60-day attrition dropped dramatically.

Once an employee passes the 60-day mark and you are fairly comfortable with how they are performing and have addressed any opportunities in a positive manner and recognized them for some wins in that first 60 days, you then need to move on to retention of them as a regular employee and not as a new hire. With any employee at this point over 60 days or at 6 years you want to understand that the longer you keep them around the better it is for you and your business. While that may sound like I'm being captain obvious with that statement let's look at some facts that tie to that statement. For this example, I'll use my current employer's numbers and while these may be different for you they are fairly universal and can be adjusted with your best estimates based off your annual sales and staff.

Currently when we hire someone there are two main cost buckets that are attached to this, hard costs and soft costs or opportunity costs. The hard costs would be items such as the drug testing, background checks, legal form retentions, training materials, payroll to complete training and orientation, payroll to cover interview days, new associate handbooks, supplies, uniforms, etc. Our current hard cost is roughly $500 when we factor everything in and that is just to get them in the door and never interact with an item or customer. Our current soft costs include some unknowns or opportunity costs, so you have to take your best guesstimates here, but we come out with $5,000 per vacant position if filled within 14 days and closer to $10,000 depending on the actual position. The soft or opportunity costs are things like lack of productivity between the last employee and the next employee hitting the floor, the lack of sales and product knowledge that can take weeks or longer to get up to speed on, the lack of comfort of that employee engaging with a customer confidently and closing a sale, the lack of awareness of the services you offer that a more tenured employee would much easier offer to a customer. While your number may be higher or lower depending on your annual sales volume if you look at mine at a cost of $500 to our bottom line profit and a cost of at least $5,000 to our top line sales it is a much bigger deal to try and make sure my employees are happy and comfortable in their positions. If you use these numbers and on a staff of 150 employees with a 33% attrition rate that would be 50 employees a year in turnover and at a cost of $5,500 that is a $275,000 hit to my store, if attrition is at 50% then it's a $412,500 hit to my store! I assure you it is worth my time and efforts to engage with my employees in aisle and do the weekly check ins and monthly town halls to help keep people happy to lower that attrition cost and raise overall sales just by retaining tenured employees. Please look at your time with your employees as an investment in their future and not as a cost or a burden so you can avoid the attrition pitfalls and reap the retention benefits.

As I am looking to retain these employees a few of the tips and tricks I mentioned above I want to elaborate on further here. Obviously, a leader who is engaged and comes out of their office to engage with their people is much more likely to have a personal relationship and know when someone is not happy or themselves. I use this knowledge to get in front of issues before they turn into bigger opportunities and get to the point that they would no longer want to work at my location. Another thing that I mentioned was using town halls, a town hall is where you bring back 4 or more employees from a variety of positions and tenures to give you "anonymous" feedback on what is going well, what is not going well, and who they would like to recognize in the store. I like to ask for three positives or things to "Keep doing", three negatives or opportunities to "Stop doing" or change, and then one individual to recognize. That individual that you go recognize takes a lot of pride when they know their peers told the leadership that they were doing a great job and the employees who suggested that individual feel good that they were able to help a peer get recognition they deserved.

If you take the town hall serious and look to keep doing and expand on the things that your team values then you will have a lot higher retention and associates will feel a lot more comfortable to come to you with issues as they arise in the moment since they know that you truly care and are not doing the meetings because you have to, but that you want to. I want to make it very clear though to take advantage of the opportunity issue and actually take action and don't ever try to throw out a response or reasoning for why things they don't like are the way they are. If they give you a negative, your role as the leader is to come up with a solution that helps turn that negative into a more positive light if not all the way to a positive.

One great example I would use for this is I had two town halls in a row where I had comments on the cleaning crew not doing a thorough job in the women's restroom and the frustration that the female employees were having. As a male leader I did not regularly (if ever) step foot into the women's restroom and had I not had these town halls to bring it up and they had not brought it to my attention otherwise this could have gone on for months without action and both employees and customers would have felt we didn't care. I immediately set up a meeting with the cleaning crew to cover expectations and made it clear that I would not allow another complaint of my team to happen and I would be switching crews if they could not live up to the expectations we had in place. The cleaning crew was very responsive and changed out the individual who was not doing the job correctly and not only did I not get another complaint from any of my female employees, I in fact actually started to get compliments from them asking if we had done something different since there was a noted change from before. A simple meeting and conversation lead to a solution for an unknown problem that showed I would take actions and fix things brought to my attention. This helped build trust and loyalty from my employees and helped with harder or more specific issues being brought up individually as well as in future town halls. Once your employees know they can trust you and you will take action on things that matter to them you will be able to retain them to a much higher degree.

I wrote earlier in the book about getting to know your people on a more personal basis and will write later about finding what motivates them, but these both come down to creating a culture in your business. You want your people to say confidently that they trust their leaders, that they care about them, that they care about their families, that they are here to see the team succeed and not just there for their own paycheck. This is creating a culture of positivity and will go a long way to building momentum of associates excited to work with you and not even consider looking elsewhere. Whenever you have an employee past a year in position that is looking to leave for something other than a move or promotion they are generally leaving for a reason. As a leader you have to try to not give them any reasons to leave you and even begin looking for a new job. People past one year in position leave leaders, not jobs. Create a culture of openness in your environment where they feel valued, respected, trusted, empowered, and that you are there for them and you will not face near the attrition levels you would should you not live up to those values.

Chapter Twenty
Recognition and Rewards

As a leader one of the most important things that you can do is have a clear and consistent form of recognition and rewards for your people. People by nature crave validation for their hard work and the efforts that they have put into the results being delivered. Your role in this in the recognition and rewards in your business is to be the key driver but not necessarily the only person involved, in fact I would say that you should only be a part of the recognition process and work to involve as many employees in it as possible for them to feel a part of the team and helping to be able to show their feedback matters and that they have a voice.

One of the ways that most leaders fail at the most is the day to day high fives and thank-yous to their teams as they are working and delivering on goals, assignments, challenges etc. An employee expects their work to get noticed both positive and negative and unfortunately most leaders are more hardwired as a manager in this situation and fall too far to the side of managing by exception that they only ever provide the negative feedback or call out what wasn't done or even just start handing out a new set of assignments before you stop to recognize the employee for what they have done and thank them for getting it accomplished. I can tell you that a thank you and a high five or a handshake are both free and will actually get you a lot more clout in the eyes of your employees if you use them on a regular basis and are truthful in your appreciation. Make sure to do these recognitions in public whereas many people as possible will see them and will help show off your recognition to as many employees and customers as possible when it makes sense. Make time to stop and thank your people or they will believe that you do not care about them and their contributions and that is unfair to everyone involved.

The next thing I like to use in my recognition and rewards process is to involve peers whenever possible. A recognition that comes from a peer or a group of peers can sometimes hold more value than even the praise of you their leader because it is unexpected, and they aren't trying to please their peers. I like to allow employees to do monthly voting for employee of the month, to use our "Kudos!" program to place a written thank you to a peer on a "Kudos!" card and place it on a recognition board in our breakroom where every employee in the store can see and read it as well. This is a fantastic program because it stays up there until you take it down and can be seen and read multiple times by multiple employees and is not a one-time benefit to your recognition program. The more employees feel they have a voice and are valued in the recognition the better performance they will generally deliver, and they are more likely to provide unsolicited recognition in the future because you have then built a culture in your business where that is the norm and a routine experience.

Another thing that I use in my recognition and rewards process are hand written thank you notes for top performers when they exceed certain sales goals, certain milestone achievements, or multiple customer compliments for just a few examples. These handwritten thank you notes can be taped to lockers, handed to the employee in person, or even sometimes mailed to the employee's home for a bit more of a dramatic effect. I once mailed a thank you note to the family of one of my most valued employees thanking them for allowing their mother to spend so much time with us at the store and that they should be proud of her for being such an important member of our team.

The day after the employee received the note at home she came in almost in tears and hugged me saying that her husband and kids could not believe that I had sent the note and raved about what a great person she must be at work to get this award and recognition sent to them. She had so much more pride in that moment than any amount of verbal praise or recognition could have provided. I also then heard about it from other employees for what a great idea that was and they couldn't wait till they received one of their own someday.

Another way to use written recognition is to hand out personalized congratulations cards to all employees when they hit a yearly milestone with the company or a birthday card for their birthday. This is a harder process the more people that you have but is a great one to let your people know that you value and care about them as individuals and not just as employees. You have to do this for everyone, not just top performers though so if you do it then commit to it and do not miss a single one. I have my HR assistant give me a monthly list for all birthdays and anniversaries for the coming month, so I can have the cards ready to go and hand signed by me and their other leaders if possible. While this may be a hard process it is absolutely worth the efforts and will pay dividends all year long.

Another tool I use for recognition is a breakroom monitor presentation that plays from a USB drive on a monitor in the breakroom 24/7. The presentation is filled with fun facts, training information, sales milestones and overall business information, benefits information, the monthly birthday and anniversary announcements in addition to the cards I just discussed, as well as a few "meet the leaders" slides. The meet-the-leaders slides are fun facts about each leader in the building so all new and old employees will hopefully see a fun fact on there they can relate with and will help make them more "human" to the employees as well knowing what they like to do outside of work. I have on mine that I have a wonderful wife and daughter at home, that I am a huge Denver Broncos fan, that I'm a huge classic car guy, that I invest in cryptocurrencies, and that I enjoy fishing for fun, among about 15 more fun facts. The goal of these fun facts is to find a way for that employee to connect to me as a person and not as just the leader and then we can engage in more "fun" conversations on the floor. This then will lead to many future follow-up conversations where we can connect, and the employee will feel "recognized" when I do so. The presentation could easily be built to your liking and business needs and should take no more than 15-20 minutes a month to update and resave as a slideshow or video file to play on a loop on that monitor. Set a calendar alert reminder to update it every month on day one so you never fall behind.

The next thing to discuss is some forms of rewards that you can provide for your people. Rewards can be anything from an extra 5-15 minute break for a day, maybe writing their schedule for a week, maybe you covering their station or area while they take that extra break, maybe a candy bar and or soda, maybe a cash bonus if you have the ability to do so (even if a small amount), maybe a pizza party for the whole team or just a top department, maybe a gift card to Starbucks or a local fast food place, maybe even you washing their car for a big accomplishment! As you can see there is a never-ending list of things that you could come up with to provide rewards to your people whether on an individual basis or as a team. When you do commit to doing a reward and if you have a set goal attached to them receiving the reward when they hit it then make SURE that you pay attention and follow through. The WORST thing that you can do is promise a reward and then not deliver on it because you forgot or no longer want to for whatever reason. If you agree to something, then do it! I will tell a story of one of my mentors that taught me this back in the day that will help illustrate this a bit better.

Chester who was my mentor in this situation was a store manager for a Walmart for the situation in this story. Chester had challenged his teams to select an item to "adopt" and go after driving sales on. Chester then agreed to throw a party for the team who sold the most of the item they adopted. One of his teams that got the most excited was the cashier team who adopted Richard Simmons cookies. Chester thought that this was a bad item and he joked with them saying that if they won that he would not only do the party but that he would get up on top of a register stand in a Richard Simmons costume during business hours and dance to the oldies if they won. The employees took it and ran with it and sold out the whole store twice before coming to Chester to ask him to order a whole truckload of cookies for the next week. Chester reluctantly did place that order even though he knew that if they didn't sell these cookies within that week they would go bad and could cost him a huge markdown, he wanted to support his team in achieving the goal they had set and help them earn the reward. While he never expected them to have a chance in hell of achieving this goal they ended up selling more than two entire truckloads of cookies in a month and wouldn't you know he ended up having to pay up on the reward that he offered and agreed to. He still carries a picture of him in that costume in his wallet that an employee had taken that day and said that that was one of the best rewards that he had ever been a part of even though he loathed Richard Simmons and those cookies he knew it wasn't about him, but it was about his people and paying up to what he had agreed to. This is a powerful example of servant leadership by helping them achieve the goal even though he didn't really want to have to do the reward portion when they won. The moral of this story is set the stretch goal and then do everything you can to empower them to achieve the goal and then own up and honor your commitment for the reward.

There will be many different kinds of rewards and recognition that you can provide to your team and which ones work the best will have to be determined through trial and error and taking some swings at things that you feel have the best chances of success. Please remember to always focus on rewards and recognition in public to get the biggest bang for your buck and return on time and money investments that goes along with it and to reprimand or redirect in private. These both go hand in hand and one without the other will not work.

The last thing that I want to touch on in this chapter is that reprimand or redirection. While you may find negative or critical feedback to be difficult and some people never fully are comfortable with it as a leader you must know that failure to hold people accountable for their performance is as good as accepting it as your standard for acceptable performance. As a high performing employee why would I ever want to continue to give my best performance and efforts if I knew that the lazy guy who works with me and delivers nowhere near what I deliver and is failing to hit any of his assignments or stretch goals is still here and allowed to deliver those poor results? Water will always follow the path of least resistance and as the leader you are responsible to set up the acceptable resistance levels and hold your people accountable to it. You can never allow a high performer to go unrecognized and even worse even if recognized to see that you don't "recognize" the poor performance of your bottom performers. Top performers will fall to the level of the average performer if there is no reason for them to stay a top performer. Please take this section to heart and make sure that you are fair and consistent with your rewards and recognition as well as reprimand and redirect as needed.

Chapter Twenty-One
Finding What Motivates

This is one of the most misunderstood things in any workplace from the leadership position and unfortunately can wreak havoc on your workforce if not figured out quickly. An unmotivated workforce has no need or desire to do better than they are currently doing, no want to promote, no nagging thought at the back of their head before they think about calling in to take the day off, no true concern for the bottom line at the end of the day when dealing with your customers and can destroy your productivity very quickly. These among many other reasons are why you truly need to understand motivation and what specifically motivates your key employees.

When you think about it I bet your first thought is that money motivates people and while that may be true in some cases it has actually been found by myself as well as many others that recognition is what motivates more people than anything including the chance of financial compensation. Now I understand the thought process of money being a top motivator as for me at times that has been a crucial motivator knowing if I could just hit this last sales goal before the half closes that I could get an extra couple thousand dollars on my end of half bonus check and that sure did motivate me at that time to go out there and go kick some ass and make sure we hit those numbers. But did I use money as a motivator to my sales associates who were not as equally compensated? To some yes and to others no, I used what I knew made each employee tick to my advantage and tailored my message of motivation to each employee as such. If I used just money as a motivator those who are not motivated by finances would have been left wanting what truly motivated them and I would not have achieved the same level of success. So... What motivates people and how do you determine it, so you can use it to your advantage? Let's take a look at a few common motivators and how to take advantage of them with your employees as well as how to identify what these motivators are by employee.

Money.

We'll start with money as a motivator as that's what first comes to most leaders' minds and what common wisdom would expect. Money will motivate those who have a desire to have more in life, they want to have more money so they can spend more. These employees will generally drive nicer vehicles, live in nicer homes, wear nicer clothes, and always are speaking of the exploits they had on their days off at the movies, clubs, vacations, or whatever else they enjoy doing. This is not always the case though and they could ride the bus and wear clothes from the thrift store and desperately want to get out of this lifestyle and step up to the next income bracket and obviously money is the way they are going to do so.

To determine who this employee is all you have to do is pay attention to them in day to day interactions and listen to what they say when you ask personal questions such as what do you enjoy doing in your off time, what do you plan to do with your bonus check, etc.... Their answers will generally lead back to doing something that requires continued cash flow to fund the lifestyle or that they really want to be able to do something more for their families such as an expensive family vacation etc.... (this same employee is also motivated by providing for their family if you take note and we will get to that.)

When you use money as a motivator you have to understand that you have to be able to back that up with cold hard cash and in some instances that just isn't feasibly possible. What if you want to motivate someone motivated by money to make an impact on a sales result or metric by the end of this week? Sure, you could offer an incentive such as a gift card, or movie tickets, or something like that in lieu of money but that's going to eat up an awful lot of your disposable income and not be sustainable over the long term if your company does not have a budget to cover these expenses. You now need to find if these employees fall into a secondary motivator category, so you can use that when money is not an option as a form of motivation.

Family.

Next let's take a look at family as a motivator. There are employees who will have this as a first priority motivator or possibly as a secondary to the money motivator as just described. These employees want to be able to spend more time at home with their family, they want to be able to provide for their family first and their wants/needs over their own, they value vacation time as time to spend with loved ones more than valuing it as time away from work to decompress.

To determine who this employee is all you have to do is pay attention to them in day to day interactions and listen to what they say when you ask personal questions such as what did you do on your days off, what's new in your home life, etc.... Their answers will generally lead back to doing something that involves their family such as taking the kids to the park, they may want to show you photos of their children or pets and talk about them in detail, they will be proud to be a family centered person and it will be obvious! This person generally will be motivated by money as well but only to fund the things they want to do for their family and value the experience of family time more than the physical items the money earned buys them.

When you use family as a motivator you have to understand that they know their family inside and out and if you genuinely want to bring them up in conversation you better get it right! If you ask about their "kids" when they only have one son or daughter, or when you ask how school is going for their children but the kids aren't old enough for school yet you lose credibility to use this as a motivator as they will then see you as someone who does not know your employees and does not value home life as much as they do. To be used properly you may need to take notes on this employee whether mentally or physically on paper that you can revert back to and genuinely have concern for this associate and their family. Imagine going up to an employee and asking about how the vacation plans are coming for an upcoming scheduled time off and they light up to tell you about the plans to road trip to Disney and that they have saved up for an entire year to do so! Now up till that date you can reference the upcoming trip, give personal opinions on what to do near the resort or on the way, and can pull off it when they come back from vacation as well by asking to see photos, asking which ride was the kids favorite, etc. Then when in between bonus-check cycles or in down times you can bring up how their personal performance affects the company and by them performing well it might allow for some extra time off for their next vacation, or maybe getting off early to start a three-day weekend with the family as a result of hitting a specific metric or sales goal. I assure you the extra couple hours off early to start spending time with the family is way more important to this employee than the couple hours of lost pay for leaving early. Again, whenever using family as a motivator be genuine and know who this employee and their family are!

Recognition.

Next, we'll take a look at recognition as a motivator. Recognition should be what you hope motivates your employees as the best thing about it is that it is FREE! These employees will always be seeking feedback on how they are doing (hoping to hear good feedback), they will want to seek you or their direct supervisors out to share with you/them sales success or exceeding metrics, they know where they stand if tracked on sales or performance goals and are very proud of where they rank. These employees should stand out pretty easily based off these traits and sometimes are even draining on you to constantly have to tell them that they are doing a good job.

To determine who this employee is again you just have to pay attention to day to day conversations and listen to what they say in their responses. When they want to talk about themselves and how good they are you will know, when they know their sales or metrics numbers better than you do then you will know, when you don't give them kudos for doing a good job and they sulk off or seem down then you will know who this employee is.

To use recognition as a motivator is really pretty easy but seems to be one of the hardest things for most leaders to do as it involves them having to tell an employee they are doing a good job. I know that doesn't sound like a hard thing to do but stop for a second and think back to your last employee level job and how many times your leader told you that you were doing a good job. I'm going to guess that it was pretty hard to recall a consistent pattern of recognition or thanks for the job well done and you were obviously someone they thought highly of as you were promoted to a leader! Think about the other employees and how much recognition they must have received, yikes.

When using recognition there is a variety of ways to utilize it properly. First, just say "thanks" for a job well done, even if it was part of their daily job functions and responsibilities. I have found thanking someone for something as basic as sweeping up their work area had a major impact and they constantly kept up on keeping the area clean from that point forward much better than if I would have ignored it and just waited for it to get dirty again and have to tell them to clean it back up. That's turning a positive act into a positive behavior and keeping the negative out of it! Thank yous are FREE and can be a verbal thank you, a high five, a handshake, a hug if they are a hugger, or whatever you see fit. With this being a free motivator, it doesn't make sense why we wouldn't see more of it in the workplace other than leaders not willing to admit that their people are doing a good job even if they think they can do better. Sometimes giving kudos and thanks for doing something right will turn around an employee's poor results a lot faster than disciplining them for not doing whatever it is they are struggling with. The last point I want to make on using "Thanks" as a motivator is to always "Do it in Public"! That might sound funny, but I have found it catchy when teaching new leaders how to do it, so they can get full effect of the recognition. If you thank an employee while they are by themselves, they will feel good, but it will go by quickly and will be forgotten if another one is not given in a fairly quick time frame. If you "Do it in Public" and make sure there is a crown around of their peers preferably it will have a much larger impact and they will remember it for days to come if not longer and will almost certainly be dinner table conversation later with the family to boast and brag about how they were told what a good job they were doing in front of their entire department, store, division, etc.... The other benefit of doing it in public is that the other employees that were present are now wanting to get that same recognition and will want to do better so that they can have that happen to them sometime in the near future. What a win-win strategy that will again cost you nothing but time!

Second if you do not have a company specific form of recognition then you need to come up with one on your own. I have used things such as the "Kudos!" cards where a great act an employee did was written on the card and posted in a common workplace area such as a breakroom for all other employees to see, or milestone awards such as being bronze, silver, gold, and platinum award winning employees based off hitting different sales or metrics results that would be presented to the employee by their leader for a job well done and then challenged/motivated to try and hit the next level, or something like a "Ring the Register" or "Cha-Ching! Check" award where you print out a copy of a big-ticket sale on a fake check and present for the employee to hang in their personal work space as a badge of honor for closing a big sale! Imagine an employee's morale and motivation when they walk to their area and see a wall covered in these sales milestone awards or checks showing that they are a top performer not to mention making it pretty easy for you as the leader to use these awards every time you walk by to thank them for a job well done and if dated on the award look to see when the last award was so you can challenge/motivate them to hit the next level or put up another award by the next time you come by.

Recognition should be easy and should be practiced regularly especially by those who care more about being told they are doing a good job than how much money they make. If you fall off you can pick back up on this quickly but will lose value if you don't bring consistency to the award levels if given at a set metric or sales goal, etc. If you commit to a recognition strategy stick to it!

Promotion/position of power.

Next, we'll take a look at promotion/position of power as a motivator. Promotion is a wonderful thing within companies as these employees know what it's like to do the position below them and can relate to the daily struggles that employees face and can help bring tried and true processes to keep things on track. The next great thing about employees motivated by promotion is that they will always be striving to be better than they are now, to do more than is required from their current job description and pay rate, and in a financial aspect these employees are generally promoted at a lower wage than if you hired someone off the street to do the position and with whatever raise comes with it will bring a piece of the money motivator factor along with it. These employees will always be seeking out stretch assignments and things that they can do extra in down time or things they can learn to do the job at a higher capacity than others, they will want to seek you or their direct supervisors out to share with you/them sales success or exceeding metrics and ways they are directly impacting the results as a leader, they see themselves as a leader amongst their peers and will let it be known that they want to lead projects or assignments when given the opportunity. These employees should stand out with both physical body language in a crowd as well as verbal when given the opportunity to speak on department or store topics they directly impact.

To determine who this employee is other than what was just listed above you should recognize the desire to move up within the company in day to day conversations when they ask about open positions, what it took for you to get to where you are, what training and schooling is required for the next positions etc. These associates will generally be very upfront about their desires to promote or be in a position of power and won't have to have it drug out of them by a bunch of questions on your part. These employees value your time and attention to help them learn more than the prospect of the next annual pay raise or bonus check as they want the big jump in pay to come along with the promotion they seek.

To properly utilize promotion or positions of power as a motivator you have a few options to implement. First you need to determine the ability of this employee to take on the next level of leadership position and tailor your strategy based off this. If this employee is seen as someone with potential you will want to take advantage of that to start them on the path of training and development as early as you can, even if they are not promoted for a year or more later if they see they are being given the training and tools to do it when the opportunity arises they will constantly be doing more than is required and will have hope for the future. If you determine that this employee is far off from being ready or just don't think that they have the skills and ability to do so you can still use this desire to promote to your advantage. Can this employee be given small bits of training and assignments with minor power to help them determine where they truly stand? If not, then you may have to have that upfront conversation about where they stand and outline steps they can take over an extended time to get themselves into a position for more training opportunities and put some of the development onto them.

Once you determine that this employee has true potential and merits you will want to do some personal one on one time with them in your office to discuss their future and how you can help them get to where they want to go. This will take some time planning on your part but the fact that you pulled them into your office to speak to them personally about their future will light a fire in that associate that will burn as long as you feed the flame in that employee. You should discuss what they want to do in the near and long-term future, you should discuss what they are currently doing to help themselves get to that next level, you should then create a 30-, 60-, 90-day game plan or 3-, 6-, 9-month game plan for that employee to use to better prepare themselves for that next position. Once you implement this game plan you need to give this employee opportunities of power such as leading the next reset team, organizing a game plan for an underperforming area in the store, coming up with an adopt an item program where they can pick a product to drive for the duration of their game plan to track effectiveness of strategy and discuss changes to strategy made if progress was not on track, etc.. This employee will be motivated to come in early, stay late, do whatever it takes to get the job done and in the best possible way, so they can prove that they should be the next to promote when opportunity arises. You must be consistent with this employee and ask them about progress on their game plans as you see them at work, you must set up calendar alerts to remind you to discuss progress of their plans, etc. When you show your dedication to them they can and will be a true asset to your company!

Sense of accomplishment.

Next, we'll take a look at sense of accomplishment as a motivator. Sense of accomplishment is a generally a motivator trait of the newer workforce (Millennials) as they want to know that what they are spending their time on actually means something and working for a company that cares about the community and environment as much or more than they care about the bottom line. While this will not be a top one you come across you should be aware of it as it may or may not expand as the millennial workforce continues to grow. These employees will generally be younger and a bit easier to identify as a result. These employees will sometimes seek feedback on how they are doing as a person and as part of the team but will generally want you to approach them more than them wanting to approach you, they will want to know overall impacts on the organization such as how well your store is performing in comparison to district or market, they enjoy group recognition where everyone gets a piece of the credit for what was accomplished. This employee should be pretty easy to determine falling into this category based off these above traits.

To properly utilize a sense of accomplishment as a motivator you just need to include these employees in the overall impact on the results of their department, store, district, etc. When you discuss the overall accomplishments and are able to tell them how what they did was a part of those results they will feel that sense of accomplishment they desire. When you post some of the "Thank you" style awards as discussed prior directed to them or their department they will feel that sense of accomplishment. When you deliver their yearly performance review and are able to articulate what impact they had as an individual and as a member of the overall group they will feel that sense of accomplishment. These employees just want to belong and know that whether fully true or not that they really matter to the company and if they were not around it would be worse off for your location. These employees are also generally eco and socially conscious and will want to hear you talk about what the company as well as you as their leader do for the community and the environment. These could be conversations about things such as instituting a recycling program if one does not currently exist in the common areas or asking them to lead a volunteer project to give back to the community, or even asking them to teach a class to your customers that would allow them to engage on a more personal level. You will find this one likely the hardest to positively impact on a day to day basis and as such really need to find what secondary thing motivates this employee the most and use that to keep these employees happy. I have found that generally the most common secondary motivator for these employees is the recognition group and while they have a lot of overlap the big difference is this employee cares more about the group recognition and how they played a part than the personal recognition that the other basic "Recognition" group seeks more directly.

Fear.

Next let's take a look at fear as a motivator. These are employees who will require a little bit of fear to keep them on their toes and motivated and strangely enough as it may sound they actually enjoy the fact of overcoming that fear when they show they can perform well. I would say this one applies to almost all employees at one time or another and especially as employees become more tenured and complacent in their positions. I would bet even you the reader fall into this category at times. These employees want to be able to be challenged to do more and, have the bar raised, and know that you see what they are doing. These employees value the fact that they can face adversity and overcome it and then feel great pride when they are able to exceed expectations given to them.

To determine who this employee is you have to pay attention to them in day to day interactions and listen to what they say as you have personal conversations, observe their efforts as they receive challenges, watch to see employees who appear to be bored at times, etc. These employees need to be challenged and need their leaders to put pressure on them to rise to the occasion. Think back to teenagers who could be told to clean their room a thousand times and may or may not do it and when they do they half ass it and then think about how when you threaten to take away the cell phone or Wi-Fi password how the fear motivated them to put some true efforts into the task at hand. The way these people were raised sometimes hard wires this into these employees as the only way for them to care about doing more than the basic expectations.

When you use fear as a motivator you have to understand that these employees think different from most and that even though they may want or need a "kick in the ass", a "come to Jesus" conversation, or even just a stern honest conversation they don't do it as a result of not wanting to do well or at times even on purpose. Many times, these employees are just bored and not feeling challenged, overly confident with their performance, or complacent with mediocrity. I'll use an example from my own past when I was an assistant manager and my store manager was walking me through the store and was beating me up left and right about all the little nit-pick things he could come up with as we went through the store such as dirt under the racking, crooked price stickers on the shelves, random empty spots on the shelf and when he finished he told me that he would be re-walking it the next day and expected immediate results and disciplinary actions would happen if it wasn't up to his standards. I was pissed as the store was beating sales plan, top to operating profit in our district, and had some of the best customer service scores in our region. I didn't understand why he was being so hard on me despite all the positive results we were putting up until I stepped back and looked at it from the point of view that I would normally not allow these small issues to stack up and as a result of the great results I myself had become complacent and was not leading with a sense of urgency. Worse than that I had allowed my employees to know that I had dropped my expectations and allowed them to get away with being mediocre. I sure worked an awful lot harder that night to get it right and I sure kept on my toes and lead with a greater sense of urgency over the coming months for fear of having that walk happen again and fear that my leader had the thought that I was not trying my hardest. I wouldn't say fear is my motivator, but I would say that given in the right doses to all associates as they show they need it is always a good recipe for success as long as you balance it along with the recognition piece as well.

Now that you have a good idea of some of the top motivators you can look for them amongst your team as you listen to them and pay attention to who they truly are. Once you begin to determine which factors motivate them you can put them into mental categories, so you know how to properly pull more out of them in the future as needed. You will waste your time and lose morale and effectiveness if you try to do a one-size- fits-all motivation process, make sure you know what motivates on an individual basis as well as in general by department or group/shift/etc. While these are the top ones I have seen in my career history I can tell you that they are definitely not a definitive list and you will have to create additions to these groups as you engage with your teams on an individual basis. You may find one is motivated by perks such as food in the office on Fridays, or casual wear workdays, or something along those lines (this is another big one but only find it to be effective when used in moderation due to general budget restrictions on providing food on a regular basis). You may find one is motivated by having fun and they want to come up with games and team build exercises to stay motivated. You may find one is motivated by socialization and just wants to be able to come to work and meet new people and have different experiences every day. You may find one is motivated by music and when you change the stations they drop off in productivity, etc. As long as you are on the lookout for personal traits and things that bring out the best in your people you will be able to motivate them based off of that as long as you can tie that motivation factor back to a job process or deliverable.

Lastly on this topic as the leader it is solely YOUR responsibility to INSPIRE and MOTIVATE your employees, not their responsibility to show up and do a good job. If you expect more out of your people than you are willing to put into inspiring and motivating them, then you will fail, and I can assure you of that. Best you can hope for without increasing employee motivation is being mediocre and as a leader that will lead to mediocre room to continue to climb your corporate ladder, mediocre room to achieve financial success, and mediocre reasons for high performing employees to want to stay working for you and your company. No one ever hired on anywhere with the intention to do a bad job, you saw something in them when you hired them and if they struggle it's your responsibility to pull them back into the right lane and get them back excited to be on your team. Remember, as a leader it is not about you, it is about your people!